The Impact of Short-Term Missions on Long-Term Missional Development

EVANGELICAL MISSIOLOGICAL SOCIETY MONOGRAPH SERIES

Anthony Casey, Rochelle Scheuermann, and Edward L. Smither
SERIES EDITORS

A Project of the Evangelical Missiological Society

www.emsweb.org

The EMS Monograph Series publishes the best book length works of EMS members. The monographs may be reworked dissertations or original works based on missiological research focused on aspects of history, theology, culture, strategy, or spiritual formation all relating to the academic and practical nature of the missionary enterprise. EMS monographs are peer reviewed and authors work with an editing team from Pickwick Publications (Wipf and Stock). Typically, 3–5 monographs are published each year.

The Impact of Short-Term Missions on Long-Term Missional Development

BRIAN BAIN

foreword by
R. Daniel Shaw

PICKWICK *Publications* · Eugene, Oregon

THE IMPACT OF SHORT-TERM MISSIONS ON LONG-TERM MISSIONAL DEVELOPMENT

Evangelical Missiological Society Monograph Series

Pickwick Publications
An Imprint of Wipf and Stock Publishers
199 W. 8th Ave., Suite 3
Eugene, OR 97401

www.wipfandstock.com

PAPERBACK ISBN: 978-1-6667-8868-6
HARDCOVER ISBN: 978-1-6667-8869-3
EBOOK ISBN: 978-1-6667-8870-9

Cataloging-in-Publication data:

Names: Bain, Brian, author. | Shaw, R. Daniel, foreword.
Title: The impact of short-term missions on long-term missional development / by Brian Bain ; foreword by R. Daniel Shaw.
Description: Eugene, OR : Pickwick Publications, 2024 | Series: Evangelical Missiological Society Monograph Series | Includes bibliographical references.
Identifiers: ISBN 978-1-6667-8868-6 (paperback) | ISBN 978-1-6667-8869-3 (hardcover) | ISBN 978-1-6667-8870-9 (ebook)
Subjects: LCSH: Short-term missions. | Missions—Theory.
Classification: LCC BV2063 B35 2024 (print) | LCC BV2063 (ebook)

To my wife Hailey, not a second goes by that I am not thankful we tied the double-knot. Thanks for supporting my dreams by always letting me chase them.

Contents

List of Tables

List of Tables

Foreword

R. DANIEL SHAW

TRAINING FOR MISSIONAL SUCCESS

As a MISSION AVIATION Fellowship board member for 18 years, it warms my heart to read Brian Bain's introduction. He tells how Nate Saint, a pilot with MAF in Equator, a martyr for the sake of attempting to communicate the gospel to a group of jungle dwellers, and a testimony of appropriate training that had life-long missional impact, set Bain on a search for effective missional engagement. Thank you Brian for giving me the joy of participating in your doctoral research, sharing your story and presenting material that will benefit the Church of Jesus Christ as we seek to partner with God for the sake of humanity being in relationship with a God who cares about us all.

Anthropologists love models that assist in organizing data to enable understanding of cultural contexts. Ward Goodenough, a longtime anthropologist at the University of Pennsylvania, (who encouraged me as I was anticipating research in Papua New Guinea) developed a research model I have often used. Initially, Goodenough focused on establishing what is, he called it "identity," appreciating what identity means as a cultural ideal, what he called "status," and understanding the difference between what is and what should be which he called "role". The reality of how people actually live out the difference between the ideal and the real, was where Goodenough positioned anthropological research; what we need to know in order to behave appropriately and thereby interact effectively within a cultural context—wherever we may find ourselves.[1]

1 Goodenough, "Rethinking."

Though Bain does not specifically use this model, at a conceptual level identifying what Short Term Mission (STM) is all about, provides an important identity he establishes in Part I. In Part III he utilizes his research to present a new ideal for capitalizing on the "disorienting dilemma" a STM creates—what could be if we find the means to capture that moment for life-long missional impact. Moving from what is to the ideal is where his research in Part II takes him. The resultant charts and graphs clearly present his findings. They reflect his excellent application of research methods to understanding the ideas, feelings, and actions of SMT, both for those who "go" and those who engage with outsiders for "mutual benefit." This research creates a critical bridge to establishing a rationale for change on the one hand and a new approach to capturing the experiences on both sides of the STM engagement in order to mobilize people for mission. Again, I congratulate Bain on the success of communicating this process of learning, application and implementation for affecting STM engagement.

As an anthropologist, I enjoy synthesizing research from specific contexts and generalizing to models that can help the broadest possible audience. Thus, Bain's work suggests the value of another model often characterized as the "E-scale". Developed by Ralph Winter in association with unreached people groups[2] and later used by Peter Wagner in the context of Church Growth Theory,[3] the model recognized the role of cultural distance in the success of evangelism. The closer the evangelist is to those who are evangelized, the greater the likelihood of people understanding the message and applying it to their lives.[4] Thus cross-cultural evangelism with the need for extensive learning prior to entry into the context, culture and language learning in the context, and the years necessary to assimilate it all for effective gospel communication, is a complex enterprise fraught with much difficulty.[5]

What Bain is suggesting, in this book, is that initial training for the STM context, engaging in partnership with the people and experiencing the disorientation that often results from cross-cultural interaction, produces the transformation which, if appropriately captured and maximized, will result in effecting mono-cultural evangelism in the context close to home. Hence his thesis is that STM trips "provide an opportunity for

2. Winter, "Finishing."
3. Wagner, *Crest*.
4. Winter, "Finishing."
5. Shaw, "Culture and Evangelism."

transformative growth for all involved, particularly the trip participants."[6] As participants engage in intentional post trip follow-up in the Mission Academy (MA) sessions, discipling precipitates transformation that captures the missional moment and lasts a lifetime. His careful step by step suggestions for designing STM and MA in order to ensure progressive change for all who participate, captures the value of the disorienting dilemma and moves participants toward a lifetime of missional engagement. For me this is the takeaway of the entire book. And for Bain, transformation "is about making meaning out of experiences and questioning assumptions based on past experiences."[7]

Thus, while not saying so, Bain is expressing Goodenough's recognition of the contrast of what is, and what could be to create a new paradigm for benefiting from what has often been maligned and even deplored by academics writing about "Christian tourism" as STM has often been characterized.[8] Bain manages to capture the problem, seeks to understand the reality and grasp the possibility of managing STM for the sake of God's kingdom on earth as it is in heaven. I draw your attention to his progression of thought, his presentation of the data and the development of a new approach to enhancing transformation. Again, I congratulate him on his insight.

Finally, a biblical perspective to reinforce Bain's message. The usual presentation of the "Great Commission" in Matthew 28, is to emphasize the word "go". The agency is on those who go and then utilize Jesus's message in order to be effective, even to the ends of the world—or is it to be obedient until the end of the age? However, your theology dictates, the focus is on the evangelist as the agent—the one who goes. In Acts 1:4–6, there is a distinct shift of agency. The messenger is energized by the Holy Spirit to be a "witness," one who passes on what has been experienced utilizing the power of the Holy Spirit to present the name of Jesus as the only way to God (John 14:6). This change of agency, with its emphasis on "being" a witness of the risen Christ, rather than "doing" ministry for Jesus, captures Bain's progression with its shift from "going" on a STM to "witnessing" in a context. The context also shifts from "out there" in Matthew, to "stay here" in Acts. Of course, verse four is often used as a message for sending missionaries into "all the earth," but before the apostles went to Judea, Samaria

6. Bain, *Impact*, chapter 2.
7. Bain, *Impact*, chapter 2.
8. Priest, *Effective*. Howell, *Ethnography*.

and all the world, they were told to stay, to wait, to utilize their cultural heritage, to witness to God's power in ways that made sense to all who heard it as we see in Acts 2:12. For Jesus's disciples, the focus was on obedience which brought transformation by way of God's presence with them and their message was valuable for their context. Later, when they became comfortable and established in Jerusalem, God moved them out through persecution but that's another story.

To Bain's point, the value of transformative learning theory optimized by a disorienting dilemma enhanced by the pre-trip—trip—post-trip progression, changes the STM experience from a colonial expression of benevolence to a mutual expression of discipleship emerging from mutually beneficial relationships in a ministry context—each side benefits and learns from the expertise of the other. This mutuality continues long past the trip so long as the change is nurtured through a process that captures the expressions into a new ideal of witness within the missional context of the environment for both the traveling messenger and the benefitting partner. To this end, "STM participants cannot be governed by a drive to accomplish something to the point of doing damage instead of good. The narrative needs to change from Americans going to help people overseas to broken people coming together for mutual, long-lasting benefit."[9] I commend Bain for his research, development of thought, and insights for change that will have a dynamic impact on short-term mission and long-term missional engagement. Furthermore, I commend the book to you for implementation in your STM engagement and the resulting commitment to mission. Enjoy the read!

R. Daniel Shaw
Sr. Prof. of Anthropology and Translation
Fuller Seminary School of Mission and Theology
Pasadena, California
June, 2023

BIBLIOGRAPHY

Bain, Brian. *The Impact of Short-Term Missions on the Long-term Missional Development of Participants.* Eugene, OR: Pickwick Publications, 2024.
Goodenough, Ward H. "Rethinking Status and Role: Toward a General Model of the Cultural Organization of Social Relationships." In *The Relevance of Models for Social Anthropology*, edited by Michael Banton, 1–24. London: Tavistock, 1965.

9. Bain, *Impact*, Conclusion: Recommendations for STM.

Howell, Brian M. *Short-Term Mission: An Ethnography of Christian Travel Narrative and Experience*. Downers Grove, IL: IVP Academic, 2012.

Howell, Brian M. "Is Your Trip Tourism or Mission?" *Christianity Today*, September 18, 2019. https://www.christianitytoday.com/ct/2019/october/dont-paint-orphanage-short-term-mission-trips-debates.html.

Priest, Robert J. *Effective Engagement in Short-Term Missions: Doing It Right*. Pasadena: William Carey Library, 2008.

Shaw, R. Daniel. "Culture and Evangelism: A Model for Missiological Strategy." *Missiology* 18 (1990) 291–304.

Wagner, C. Peter. *On the Crest of the Wave: Becoming a World Christian*. Ventura: Regal, 1983.

Winter, Ralph A., and Bruce D. Koch. "Finishing the Task: The Unreached People's Challenge." In *Perspectives on the World Christian Movement: A Reader*, edited by Ralph Winter and Stephen Hawthorne, 531–46. Pasadena: William Carey Library, 2009.

Winter, Ralph D. "The Highest Priority: Cross-Cultural Evangelism." In *Let the Earth Hear His Voice*, edited by J. D. Douglas, 213–25. Minneapolis: World Wide, 1975.

Abstract

IN THIS BOOK, I address the need for post-trip training and discipleship following a short-term mission trip. To address this need, I reviewed the literature relating to short-term missions and transformative learning theory. In my review, I found that short-term mission literature is full of valuable content regarding preparing participants for a trip and even conducting a trip, but when it came to post-trip follow-up there was very little material. The transformative learning theory literature served as a very insightful frame for me to evaluate and later offer suggestions for short-term mission practitioners. This review of the literature led to my field research.

My research involved unstructured interviews, open and closed surveys, and participant observation. I interviewed both U.S. short-term mission participants and South Sudanese pastors. The surveys were entirely from U.S. participants from various churches and organizations who had travelled to South Sudan. The research examined the short-term mission experience through each of the pre-trip, trip, and post-trip phases. Through this research I come to the conclusion that not only is there a great gap in the literature but also in the popular practice of short-term missions in regard to post-trip follow-up training.

I believe that this gap represents an incredible lost opportunity in terms of discipleship and missionary development. My proposed solution is to apply transformative learning theory and adult learning practices to design short-term mission experiences in a way that better captures the disorienting dilemma of the short-term mission trip. This involves a new level of intentionality on the part of sending organizations and trip leaders to design a discipleship-oriented learning experience that transcends the actual trip itself. I also provide a model for post-trip discipleship that I call Missionary Academy. Missionary Academy seeks to help people live active

Abstract

missional lives in their home contexts by becoming gospel fluent in the context of a gospel-centered community.

Acknowledgments

FOR THE BOOK YOU now hold in your hands, there is no shortage of people that I want to thank. I want to begin with my wife Hailey. You were my great encouragement and inspiration in making the decision to apply for the doctoral program that led to the dissertation that led to this book and you never wavered throughout it, even though it meant missing your birthday every year. I have received nothing but support from you and without you standing with and beside me this book would never have been written. Thank you for believing in me.

It was through my friend Jeff Holck, that I learned about the doctoral program and had the courage to apply. I am thankful for your regular encouragement and especially your tips along the way from someone always one-step ahead. I am honored to have been able to walk the stage together. Mark Hopkins had enough faith to take on the risk of letting a relative rookie into a respected program. I have not forgotten and I hope you have been proud of the outcome. Betsy Glanville was an essential piece in my dissertation reaching completion and me passing my defense. Thank you for always being only an email away and for investing in the success of this dissertation as though it were your own. Through his books, Dan Shaw was a mission's hero of mine before I ever met him. It has been a great honor for me to spend four years with you and an even greater honor to have you invest a small part of your life in mine. Together, we made it happen.

I'm thankful to the Evangelical Missiological Society Monograph Series Committee for seeing value in my dissertation and sponsoring it to publication. Michael Burer and George Hillman at Dallas Theological Seminary have both been a welcome encouragement for me in pursuing publication for my dissertation. Sara Sherman and Shannon Janssen have been an enthusiastic help in preparing this manuscript for publication.

Acknowledgments

Roger and Barbara Simons have been among my strongest supporters since my first step into ministry back in 2002. Thank you for being a primary instrument of the Lord in making everything that has happened from then to now, including my doctorate and this book possible.

My Mom and Dad, Ken and Cynthia Bain have supported my education and studies since the first day they dropped me off at preschool. You sat in the stands even when I was sitting on the sidelines and helped with projects that were beyond me. Thank you for doing it all so well.

List of Abbreviations

LTM   Long-term mission

MA   Missionary Academy

STM   Short-term mission

TLT   Transformative learning theory

U.S.   United States of America

Introduction

IN 2002, I WENT on my first short-term mission (STM) trip. Since then, I have served on three different continents, experienced last minute evacuations, led teams, and travelled alone. I have had the opportunity to see some of the largest cities in the world and live in some of the most remote villages. In all of these travels, I have been blessed with some amazing relationships and the opportunity to see God work in amazing ways. As I reflect on these experiences, I cannot help but wonder about the long-term impact of so many of these short-term trips. This is especially true in regard to the trip participants from the United States (U.S.). I have long felt that current best practices in STM typically fail to capture the potential long-term impact that these trips could have on U.S. trip participants. In this dissertation, I look to discover how to best lead STM trips in a way that leads to long-term positive impact on all trip participants.

This paper recognizes the great need for the gospel-centered growth of the Church in North America and the great opportunity that STM trips offer to equip participants to better meet this need. Approximately 1.6 million U.S. adult church members travel abroad on STM each year.[1] This large number represents an incredible opportunity for mobilization and discipleship.

STM trips are a part of the evangelical framework of the U.S., particularly the Bible church movement, which is my home tradition. Depending on whom you ask, this is a great thing or a real disappointment. The argument for STM is all of the seemingly great work that happens during the trips. Whether it is the sharing of the gospel or the construction of a building, the Church is strengthened and that is a good thing. Unfortunately, it is not that simple. In recent years, great attention has been brought to the

---

1 Priest, *Effective*, ii. Numbers as of 2005

idea of STM trips often being Christian welfare in disguise. Books such as *When Helping Hurts* have shed light on this problem and done much to help the situation.[2]

These discussions leave me with the sad and even heart-breaking feeling that so much of these well-intended mission trips are truly little more than a Christian-themed adventure vacation funded by tithe money that potentially do more harm than good. The counter-argument is that the participants in the STM normally have such a life changing experience that they come home forever changed for the better. Unfortunately, I have found that is often not as true as Christians would like to think. This dissertation is my journey to discover what true value STM trips really have and what can be done to better unlock that potential.

BACKGROUND

My first STM was a pretty amazing experience and came off of one the most tangible acts of God intervening in my life that I have ever experienced. The story actually begins in the summer of 2001. After doing an internship for my degree program I resolutely came to the conclusion that sitting in a small, windowless office working with spreadsheets and receipts was not the way I wanted to spend my young adult life. After prayer and some raw courage, I decided to join the military. This was a very counter-cultural and even strange decision when compared to my peers. My classmates and most anyone else that I knew found the idea very unorthodox. To me, it seemed the perfect fit and in July of 2001 I signed up.

While this was happening, my involvement in my local church was growing a lot. STM had never been a consideration in my mind until I came upon the book *Jungle Pilot*. The book was largely a collection of journal entries from missionary pilot Nate Saint and his heart for the Lord had a deep impact on me.[3] For the first time, I dreamed of participating on an STM so I could, even if briefly, experience the depth of intimacy and joy in the Lord that Saint spoke of. My commitment to the military left no room for such a trip. I also began to experience the deepening Christian community that I had desired for years, all the time knowing it would come to an end with graduation and the military. Everything changed with the onset of 9/11 and the new world that followed. The military became overwhelmed with

2 Corbett and Fikkert, *When Helping Hurts*.

3. Hitt, *Jungle Pilot*.

candidates and I was actually released from my commitment and never served. Within two weeks, I was hired to work in the college ministry of my local church and fully supported to go on my first STM ever, to China.

The six weeks in China were fantastic. I loved the culture, the food, the adventure and significance of everything. I, and nearly everyone else on the trip, were confident we were coming back to China full-time. Out of the approximately twelve people on my team, I believe that two went back for a one or two-year short-term trip. Personally, I returned overseas the next three summers, all to Uzbekistan. In 2007, I came to Sudan[4] for the first time on a six-week trip. Two years later, I spent two months in Ethiopia followed by another month in Sudan. I now work for Small Organization A where STM is a major part of our methodology in South Sudan.

At Small Organization A, our entire strategy is built around the em-powerment of local leaders in South Sudan. Empowerment can be a tricky thing, but we are committed to it as core to our mission. The director of our organization is a South Sudanese pastor living in South Sudan. Every U.S. staff member is partnered with a South Sudanese pastor. As partners, the two work together to expand God's Kingdom, but the South Sudanese pastor always carries the final authority on the team.

I struggled with several things related to STM during these years. My first struggle was whether or not I should be a "long-term" missionary overseas or not. I was torn between what I believed was a greater service to God and what felt right to me. Despite the great value I placed on being an overseas missionary, I truly believed God was calling me to a work in the U.S. Despite this, I struggled with this tension for many years.

My second struggle with STM was how un-strategic it so often seemed. I was fortunate that all of my trips fit well into a longer-term strategy led by long-term overseas missionaries, but for so many STM trips this was not true. I am very thankful for and confident in the current method that Small Organization A uses with STM, but am constantly challenging the idea to see if things can be better. While the overseas portion of many STM trips bothered me from a strategic standpoint, what was even worse for me was how the mission ended when the trip was over. Everyone in our nation is in need of greater devotion to the Lord. As a result, there is great need for missionaries. Even so, the work of most STM participants ended when they arrived home. I always felt that that was when the work really began. It is

4. Now South Sudan, this was prior to the independence of South Sudan in July of 2011.

not necessarily exceptional to raise the bar in serving the Lord in an isolated situation overseas for a short period of time. The real challenge comes in the day-to-day living wherever participants call home. I always felt that STM was an incredible discipleship opportunity that was being missed. The STM trip itself should not be the climax of the training, but simply a key component in a bigger, intentional discipleship process.

To this day, these struggles have not gone away, but they have led me to this dissertation. I long to see STM become a discipleship engine for launching missionaries in the U.S. in a great gospel re-awakening. This dissertation captures part of my journey to expand the impact of STM.

PURPOSE

The purpose of this study is to explore how to maximize the STM experience in a way that creates the most mutually beneficial, long-term missional impact possible.

GOAL

The goal of this study is to discover best practices for structuring short-term mission experiences in a way that creates mutually beneficial, long-term missional growth in the life of participants.

SIGNIFICANCE

The significance of this study is to change the way short-term missions are conducted and followed up for the purpose of launching new missionaries throughout the U.S. and around the world. This study has impacted the way I lead trips and the way Small Organization A manages its STM trips. Presently, we have no formal process for what pre-trip training should look like and we have no expectation at all for post-trip follow-up training. As a result, there is little consistency between trips and some trip participants end up under-prepared. We also do not retain as many trip participants as involved volunteers in our ministry. The findings from this dissertation will help us to identify and resolve what is lacking in our approach.

I have discovered valuable insights, particularly regarding trip follow-up that will help promote long-term missional development in trip participants. Ultimately, I believe this study has produced results that will influence the entire spectrum of STM. I have observed a gap in many churches between pastors and missions. Many pastors have a heart for missions, but see little connection between their local church and missions overseas. STM done well has the opportunity to create a clear benefit and tie between these global and local works. For many long-term missionaries, STM has developed a burdensome and negative connotation. I believe I have found ways to reconcile and bridge this divide.

CENTRAL RESEARCH ISSUE

The central research issue is to explore the life-transformative impact of STM experiences with a special focus on the long-term missional development of trip participants.

RESEARCH QUESTIONS

1. How does STM currently operate?

2. How are participants in STM shaped by this experience?

3. Application: How can STM contribute to long-term missional development of trip participants?

DEFINITIONS

- Short-term mission – Short travel experiences for Christian purposes such as charity, service, or evangelism.[5]

- Missional living – A lifestyle where one's primary commitment is to the missionary calling of the people of God.[6]

- Missional development – A person's development in the area of missional living.

- South Sudan – The Republic of South Sudan in East Africa, which gained independence from Sudan in July 2011.

5. Howell, *Ethnography*, 20.
6. Hirsch, *Forgotten Ways*, 284.

DELIMITATIONS

- I focused specifically on STM trip participants from Dallas, Texas who went on STM trips lasting 1–2 weeks in South Sudan with Small Organization A, Large Church A, and Large Church B.

ASSUMPTIONS

- A worthwhile STM trip should be mutually beneficial for both the participant and national partners with a lasting impact for all.
- The two primary and most beneficial uses of STM are evangelism and specialized training.
- As a Christian, I believe there is absolute truth and that this belief can be compatible with various teachings that state or assume otherwise.
- All STM trip participants are from the United States and not in professional ministry.

OVERVIEW OF DISSERTATION

This dissertation explores the life-transformative impact of STM experiences with a special focus on the long-term missional development in trip participants. It begins with the introduction of the paper via the program design.

Part I of this paper is a review of the relevant literature. In Chapter 1, I will examine the current state of STM with the aim of better understanding current methods as presented in the literature and finding best practices. In Chapter 2, I will study transformative leaning theory in order to better understand the theory and its potential impact for STM.

Part II of this paper will focus on my personal field research. In Chapter 3, I will share my research methodology by explaining what I did and why. In Chapter 4, my findings and analysis of the data will be the focus.

Part III of this paper is where I will discuss my recommendations for how to move forward with STM. In Chapters 5 and 6, I will propose a new methodology for STM during the pre-trip, trip, and post-trip portions of the process. There will be a special focus on post-trip training as my research reveals that the greatest gap in current practice can be found in post-trip methodology. The dissertation will conclude with recommendations for further research.

Part I

Literature Review

PART I OF THIS dissertation consists of a review of the literature to find current popular and best practices of STM. In addition, I review definitions and popular practices of Transformative Learning Theory (TLT). The reason for studying TLT literature was to find model that could help to both evaluate and enhance the STM process. The goal is to better understand both while gaining a better picture on what best practices are for each.

Chapter 1

Short-Term Mission Methodology

IN MANY WAYS, STM is now a ministry of the church that has reached maturity. Organizations such as Cru (formerly Campus Crusade for Christ), Pioneers, and many others have very established methods of conducting STM in ways that feed long-term works and bear much fruit. In this chapter, I will examine many STM best practices to identify strengths and weaknesses. My goal is to discover best practices for the pre-trip, trip, and post-trip portions of STM.

CURRENT METHOD OF STM

The popular method of STM, as found in my personal experience as well as my review of the literature, is typically almost focused fully on the trip itself. This leads to a moderate focus on pre-trip training and essentially no follow-up training apart from some light debriefing. Even in these cases, the pre-trip training is often heavily focused on trip logistics as opposed to any particular training with a long-term mindset in view.

STM as a movement is largely made up of Christians traveling from highly resourced countries to countries with less material resources.[1] Something that tends to distinguish people on STM trips from other forms of mission is the distinct awareness of the limitations of their mission, particularly with regard to time.[2] Even with the limitations with regard to time,

---

1. Priest, "Women as Resource Brokers," 259.
2. Howell, *Ethnography*, 61.

STM can be very fruitful.[3] Rolando Cuellar defines STM as the mobilization of the church in the power of the Holy Spirit to join in God's action in the world. He goes on to say that the purpose of STM is to announce God's kingdom through brief trips with specific ministerial activities.[4]

Cuellar presents a good definition, but it seems too limiting. STM trips involve two sets of people, the goers and those being served. The focus tends to be on those presumably being served. This focus exists for good reasons, but it can be detrimental to not only trip participants, but ironically to the international hosts as well. Steve Corbett and Brian Fikkert have popularized the idea that the good intentions of North American missions can often lead to more harm than benefit in the local context.[5] This means there is no room for casually going on STM. Those going on STM must realize and accept the mutual brokenness that exists among themselves and those they are going to serve. Without this idea of mutual brokenness, the likelihood is that the work of STM will do more harm than good.[6] Corbett and Fikkert believe that one of the biggest problems in many poverty-alleviation efforts is that their methodology actually exacerbates the god-complexes of trip participants and the feelings of inferiority and shame on the part of the economically poor.[7] When trip participants embrace their mutual brokenness alongside those they are serving, the opportunity for life change is presented to everyone involved. Robert Reese describes this approach to STM as "the way of the cross" that is marked by dying to self on behalf of others. He contends that this style of STM can facilitate a style of discipleship that can pervade all areas of life.[8]

Another definition put forth for STM is: "the God-commanded, repetitive deployment of swift, temporary non-professional missionaries."[9] The authors point out that there are far too many variations of STM to arrive at one definitive definition.[10] This definition functions well and the authors' humility to acknowledge its limitations is appreciated. Even this general definition is primarily focused on the trip or "deployment" aspect

---

3. Bessenecker, "Paul's Short-Term Church Planting," 39.

4. Cuellar, "Bigger Than You Think," 278.

5. Corbett and Fikkert, *When Helping Hurts*.

6. Corbett and Fikkert, *When Helping Hurts*, 64.

7. Corbett and Fikkert, *When Helping Hurts*, 65.

8. Reese, "Spiritual Exercise," 46.

9. Peterson et al., *Maximum Impact*, 110.

10. Peterson et al., *Maximum Impact*, 110.

of STM. It is not wrong to view STM with a focus on the trip and destination, but it can lead to an imbalance that is limiting and even destructive. Limiting because it does not account well for long-term growth beyond the trip and destructive because it can exacerbate the concerns raised by Corbett and Fikkert.

I will review the three phases that exist for any STM with the goal of understanding both popular and best practices:

- Pre-trip training and preparation
- The trip itself
- Post-trip training and follow-up

In addition, three factors that need to be considered when examining STM:

- The long-term impact on STM trip participants
- The long-term impact on those they go to serve
- The mutual benefit of their interaction together

This dissertation will address all three when appropriate but the focus will be on the STM trip participants.

PRE-TRIP

The pre-trip training process is significant, Randy Friesen has found that STM participants with an extensive pre-trip discipleship training process saw significantly higher rates of lasting change compared to those who did not receive extensive pre-trip training.[11] Pre-trip training helps the STM team to adopt and create the same core narrative regarding the expectations and purpose of the shared STM experience. This shared, core narrative can be very powerful in shaping the experiences still to come.[12] Roger Peterson, Gordon Aeschliman, and Wayne Sneed identify five key pre-trip training areas: cross-cultural training, personal preparation, logistics training, intended activities preparation, and financial preparation.[13] This list is general and ambiguous enough to work well for trip preparation, but

---

11. Friesen, "Long-Term Impact," 179.
12. Howell, *Ethnography*, 123.
13. Peterson et al., *Maximum Impact*, 132.

seems to fall short of addressing the bigger picture of life change in the STM participant. Even this subtle absence runs the risk of causing harm and losing valuable long-term focus in the STM.

There are lots of versions and thoughts on what should be specifically done to prepare a team for an STM trip. I will discuss a few different perspectives and work to assimilate them into a single list. Brian Howell shares his best practices to consider for preparing a team well for an STM trip:

- Spend as much time studying the context you are going to as you do preparing for ministry activities
- Invite people from the context you are going to come and spend time with your group[14]

Howell's focus in these best practices seems to be primarily on preparing trip participants for the foreign context they will serve in.[15] Alex Smith goes beyond Howell when he says that it is important for pre-trip training to be used to help create an attitude of service and flexibility for greater effectiveness in the field.[16] Smith goes on to share several other areas of training that are important for STM participants to receive before the trip:

- Adequate long-term vision
- Selfless focus regarding impact
- Proper motivation for going
- Eternal perspective
- Healthy gospel focus
- Proper expectations with eternity in mind
- Dependence on God, healthy theology[17]

This list appears more well-rounded and has a special focus on mindset, the heart, and expectations in general. The focus on long-term vision and eternity are encouraging as it helps the participant to think beyond the trip, hopefully in terms of their own lives in addition to those they serve. The emphasis on motivation, gospel, and theology make room to promote

14. Howell, *Ethnography*, 232.

15. Howell, *Ethnography*, 232. It should be noted that Howell's book has a special focus on anthropology and not simply a "how-to" book on STM.

16. Smith, "Missiological Questions," 53.

17. Smith, "Missiological Questions," 56–57.

the essential ideas of mutual brokenness as highlighted by Corbett and Fikkert. Addressing mutual brokenness early in the pre-trip process can be helpful in preventing unnecessary harm during the trip.

Steven Ybarrola and Richard Slimbach echo the heart of Corbett and Fikkert by highlighting the importance of instilling a mindset of learning rather than doing on the part of participants. This approach is helpful in order to create the healthiest experience and opportunity.[18] STM can be an opportunity for participants to gain an understanding of anthropology that can not only help them be more aware and effective in the field, but also when they arrive back home.[19] Slimbach speaks of the importance of STM participants wrestling with the idea of what their own communities may look like if they were fully reconciled to God. This exercise is meant to help trip participants develop a well-rounded vision for the work that is needed both at home and at their trip destination.[20] Edwin Zehner adds some practical suggestions for STM trip leaders:

- Give participants assigned readings on cultures they will visit
- Provide readings and instruction on other related topics, such as poverty
- Remind participants that they are going to serve and follow, not enforce a foreign agenda
- Assign journaling tasks to promote reflection
- Hold periodic group discussions to promote dialogue
- Have people who have gone on the trip previously visit with the team before the trip[21]

I want to highlight how each list has varied notably in focus so far. Howell focused on context, Smith on the heart and mind, and Zehner seems to partially blend the two. Zehner adds the ideas of journaling and group discussions to help with processing the experience. Zehner's list also highlights how the focus on STM tends to be heavily on the STM participant more than any other group in the STM process. Rick Richardson adds the value of working to build relational and social capital among trip

---

18. Ybarrola, "Avoiding the Ugly," 104; Slimbach, "Do No Harm," 91.

19. Ybarrola, "Avoiding the Ugly," 117.

20. Slimbach, "Do No Harm," 89.

21. Zehner, "Rhetoric," 200–201.

participants as an important step toward maximizing the value of STM trips. This process begins before the trip and extends well after. One method to promote social capital is through housing trip participants together and promoting sharing and playing together. Leaders are encouraged to make it clear early to the team that strong relationships and social capital together is a high priority.[22]

In summary, I will piece together a list that reflects the value offered by each of the contributions so far. A good pre-trip training should consider including the following preparations:

- Adequate long-term vision
- Selfless focus regarding impact
- Proper motivation for going
- Healthy gospel focus
- Proper expectations with eternity in mind
- Dependence on God, healthy theology
- Assign journaling tasks to promote reflection
- Hold periodic group discussions to promote dialogue
- Spend as much time studying the context you are going to as you do preparing for ministry activities
- Provide readings and instruction on other related topics, such as poverty
- Have people who have gone on the trip previously visit with the team before the trip
- Invite people from the context you are going to come and spend time with your group

This represents a good starting point for what lessons to consider when designing a pre-trip training.

An aspect of STM that can be overlooked is recruiting and mobilizing people to serve on STM through their profession. Medical personnel typically have no shortage of opportunity to serve, but business professionals and many others often have no opportunity to directly use their gifting on STM. STM tends to offer one of two options to people: evangelism or some

22. Richardson, "Impact," 552.

form of construction, service work. This can alienate scores of people who have little or no gifting or experience in either. By identifying more ways to get people involved in STM, the opportunity to have a greater impact on people in both the U.S. and overseas grows significantly. Russell identifies six ways to get business professionals more involved in STM: seminars, training, consulting, virtual consulting, business development partnerships, and hybrids.[23] Offering service opportunities such as these not only creates the potential to recruit more people into STM, but it has the potential to open doors on the mission field as well. Many people otherwise out of reach to a missionary or pastor may open their door to a business professional offering valuable insight or training.[24] Small teams and short trips tend to offer the best scenario for specialty trips such as these.[25]

TRIP

At this point, it is important to note that there are different kinds of STM trips. Peterson, Aeschliman, and Sneed present sixteen different categories of ministry activity that can be done on STM trips.[26] I collect these into three categories of trip focus: evangelism, training, and humanitarian. According to A. Scott Moreau, in 2005, over 80 percent of STM trips were evangelism or discipleship focused, around 7 percent were humanitarian focused, and around 1 percent were training focused.[27] It was surprising to see these numbers as I expected the humanitarian focused trips to be a much larger percentage. I should note that Moreau's numbers are all from mission agencies and do not include STM trips sent out by churches. My assumption is that church sponsored trips would include a much higher level of humanitarian[28] focus, but I do not have data to confirm this. In the absence of that data, I will defer to Moreau and therefore will focus on STM trips with an evangelistic focus. An evangelistic trip can include

23. Russell, "Missional Business," 346.

24. Russell, "Missional Business," 346.

25. Russell, "Missional Business," 364–65.

26. Peterson et al., *Maximum Impact*, 71.

27. Moreau, "Missions, Inc," 16. Moreau does not specify any particular training, but does link training with education in the research cited.

28. A humanitarian focus would be one with a service orientation and no religious affiliation.

proclaiming the gospel, church planting, Bible translation, and various other kinds of outreach focused activities with a direct tie to expressing the gospel.[29]

The STM experience can serve to create a very special sense of community through the combination of the separation from normal life and the engagement in challenging new circumstances, all in the context of a new group of people. Simply by being together on the same mission, for a short time, a surprising level of camaraderie can be established. This sense of community can even transcend one trip to include others who have had similar experiences.[30]

Many times STM trips can be a challenging mix of expectation and reality. It is not unusual for trips to the developing world to have an accompanying portion of the trip that resembles that of a tourist on vacation. Expectations of surviving the developing world for a few days on STM can be dashed when participants find themselves staying in a comfortable hotel as opposed to a mud floor.[31] This, along with dedicated "tourist" times where time is spent shopping and seeing local sites can serve to put the trip participant in a bit of a paradox as to how it all fits together.[32]

Howell presents some best practices to consider for leading a team well during an STM trip:

- Spend time learning from community leaders about problems, solutions, and initiatives already in place
- Present visits to museums and historical sites as part of the mission and not simple tourist activities[33]

As with his pre-trip suggestions, Howell's focus is primarily on the anthropological and cultural. Both of Howell's points reinforce the call of Corbett and Fikkert to never lose sight of mutual brokenness and the need for mutual humility and learning.[34] Corbett and Fikkert capture this idea when they discuss how sin has impacted all people and relationships. As a result of this, all people are broken and in need of restoration. Many STM trips, often unintentionally, have the mindset that they are going to help

29. Peterson et al., *Maximum Impact*, 73.
30. Howell, *Ethnography*, 148.
31. Howell, *Ethnography*, 151.
32. Howell, *Ethnography*, 169–70.
33. Howell, *Ethnography*, 232–33.
34. Corbett and Fikkert, *When Helping Hurts*, 64.

the "poor." The assumption is that STM participants are helping the disadvantaged out of their own advantaged state. Mutual brokenness is the idea that all people are "broken" as a result of sin. Bryant Myers describes this as a brokenness that takes place with ourselves and in relation to God, others, community, and our environment.[35] When this mutual brokenness mentioned by Corbett and Fikkert is embraced, true restoration can take place on the part of everyone involved. In contrast, when mutual brokenness is not embraced, great harm can be done in the form of reinforcing and perpetuated each group's brokenness. This often means self-sufficiency and self-righteousness on the part of STM participants and dependency and low self-worth on the part of those being served.[36]

The trip portion of STM brings in some additional factors that need to be considered. An example of one of these factors is the interaction and relationship with long-term missionaries. Reports, testimonies, and opinions of STM trips being a burden on long-term missionaries serving as host are not difficult to find.[37] This issue is especially exacerbated when the STM appears to offer little or no value to the long-term mission (LTM) work. Some long-term missionaries have actually been instructed by their field leaders to keep expectations of STM trips low and see the main purpose of STM as an opportunity to mobilize for long-term field service.[38] In an attempt to help alleviate this issue, Stan May and Daniel Rickett contend that STM participants' primary role is to be servants to the LTM workers and national partners as opposed to pressing their own agenda.[39]

Ultimately, relationships are critical for mission work and STM is not an exception. Teams that return to the same areas in ongoing partnerships are more effective as this allows for long-term relationships to form.[40] Returning teams are a very helpful way to increase the value of STM to the LTM work. Having a good connection with a national on a first trip is great, but to see the depth and blessing that comes with a second trip shows the power of partnership. Bridge-building and developing relationships are paramount in effective mission scenarios.[41] With the second, and successive

35. Myers, *Walking with the Poor*, 64.

36. Corbett and Fikkert, *When Helping Hurts*, 56–64.

37. Adeney, "Myth," 121–22.

38. Smith, "Missiological Questions," 45.

39. May, "Great If...," 94; Rickett, "Partnerships," 112.

40. Smith, "Missiological Questions," 46.

41. Smith, "Missiological Questions," 50.

trips, the STM participant is able to show national and LTM partners that there is some level of commitment in place that lays a foundation for a relationship. This kind of bridge building and relationships are the means through which real impact can be had.

The role of the STM leader is critical in bringing out the best in a team.[42] Smith goes on to share some key elements of a good STM trip:

- Participants schedule ample quality time with long-term missionaries
- Personal commitment to Bible study
- Well organized training and debriefing times
- Challenging but realistic assignments
- Participants are encouraged to consider long-term involvement
- Participants understand the role they play in the bigger process
- Learn about spiritual warfare from veterans
- See the value STM plays in long-term ministry[43]

You will notice that Smith's bias comes out in that each of these recommendations focuses on the development of the STM participant. This is an appreciated transition from many of the pre-trip best practices already discussed. Even so, an imbalance is still clear.

C. M. Brown proposes several characteristics that should mark intercultural congregation-to-congregation partnerships. While such partnerships are not specifically my focus, his characteristics can be applied generally in working to create mutually beneficial relationships between STM participants and the locals they partner with while overseas. First, empowering mediation is needed. Mediators should work between the two groups to promote bridging and linking the groups to create social capital. The mediators should power dynamics and establish a system that is empowering for cooperative decision-making.[44] This would be the role of the STM trip leader as well as any LTM leaders or hosts.

Second, the partnership should be formed in a way that not only promotes, but accelerates the creation of social capital.[45] Creating social capital

42. Smith, "Missiological Questions," 47.

43. Smith, "Missiological Questions," 58–59.

44. Brown, "Friendship," 232–34.

45. Social capital carries the idea of investing in relationships, then later benefiting from that investment. By investing in someone with your time and energy, you develop a stronger relationship that will benefit you both in the future.

between the two groups should be a priority. This is where Brian Howell's tips on cultural learning are helpful as is the idea of enduring partnerships where participants return on STM again and again. Third, a system for decision-making regarding activities and resources should be developed. The decision-making process should be clear and promote the dignity of both groups. This helps to better ensure a mutually beneficial partnership. Finally, participants should be patient as the partnership develops, celebrate successes, and listen carefully.[46]

Cuellar raises several concerns about STM. For one, the brevity of the trip does not allow participants to learn the culture or language of the people. Another concern is that discipleship and commitment to Christ are pushed aside in favor of conversions and statistics.[47] This issue of brevity and culture has largely already been addressed in this dissertation. The issue of language brought up by Cuellar has not been reinforced by others sources.

Successful partnerships in missions are marked by partners from different cultures working together toward common goals based on mutual respect for each other. STM should be structured in a way that participants will be given plenty of opportunities to witness and even experience the challenges, triumphs, and struggles that indigenous leaders face. Partnerships and experiences like these go a long way toward creating a mutually beneficial encounter.[48]

The following list summarizes the best practices developed from this body of literature:

- A healthy screening process for trip participants
- Embrace the brevity of the trip
- Spend time learning from community leaders about problems, solutions, and initiatives already in place
- Participants get ample quality time with long-term missionaries
- Well-organized training and debriefing times
- Challenging but realistic assignments
- Personal growth in spiritual disciplines, including spiritual warfare

46. Brown, "Friendship," 232–34.
47. Cuellar, "Bigger Than You Think," 282.
48. Park, "Paternalism," 516.

- See the value STM plays in long-term ministry
- Mutually beneficial alignment between STM and LTM vision and mission
- STM trips should feed into a longer-term discipleship process
- STM has a focus on building relationships with nationals and LTM workers
- Present visits to museums and historical sites as part of the mission and not simple tourist activities
- Should have mediators between STM and nationals to promote a mutually beneficial scenario
- Participants are encouraged to consider long-term involvement

POST-TRIP

It is very common, if not fully normative, for lessons learned and excitement for change to fade over time once the trip ends.[49] When it comes to STM, the focus of training, preparation, and energy is typically heavily weighted toward the trip itself. When this is the case, pre-trip training is seen as playing an important role for logistics and basic preparation for the ministry and the trip itself receives much attention; it is the focus after all. In this model, the post-trip training or follow-up has little to no value apart from some debrief and very basic thoughts on transitioning back home.

Unfortunately, this is also reflected in much of the literature as the post-trip portion of STM is not something that receives much attention.[50] When follow-up is mentioned, it is typically a very brief note on cultural adjustments faced upon returning home. To begin with, there are surprisingly few books that address STM on an academic level. Many STM books serve more as a trip manual for getting people overseas with a high focus on logistics and basic dictums. I surveyed many books and resources that do not appear in this dissertation. Of those books not represented here, none addressed the post-trip portion of STM beyond a few pages on debrief and quick suggestions on becoming active in the church and evangelism upon return.

49. Howell, *Ethnography*, 226.
50. Wilder and Parker, *Transformission*, 80–83.

Howell offers some best practices to consider for post-trip training with an STM trip:

- Plan mandatory follow-up meetings to discuss lessons learned and how life is or should be as a result of the trip.

- Remember that the months after the trip are very significant in shaping the narrative of the trip moving forward.

- Make sure any presentations of the trip focus on the resources in the country and the work that is happening there as opposed to the needs there and accomplishments of the team.[51]

The three primary things that stand out here are the ideas of planning follow-up, making it mandatory, and realizing the critical role the months following the trip play. Paul Borthwick picks up on this theme and mentions the importance of weekly discipleship groups focusing on outreach and reunions following a trip.[52] Something important that is not mentioned is the need to shift the focus from the short-term to the long-term. The trip may be short, but the process and benefits do not have to be. If the trip leader makes a special focus on growth beyond the trip itself, it can help set the expectation for the team to want to continue engagement post-trip. As Howell says, post-trip follow-up cannot be left to chance but must be planned, considered mandatory, and treated with the same level of significance as the pre-trip training and even the trip itself.

STM leaders and organizations benefit by keeping the big picture in mind and remember that the impact of the trip is not the only measuring stick for STM. The growth of the participants themselves should also be considered as a potentially significant result of STM.[53] The somewhat ironic thing is that even in this article that highlights the value of STM in regard to long-term impact on participants and the value and necessity of long-term relationship, nothing is mentioned about any post-trip training beyond an initial debrief.[54] The idea of follow-up post-trip almost appears to not even be an option to be considered. Getting STM participants to commit to further training after the trip is over is no doubt a real challenge, but that just reinforces the importance of setting good expectations early on. When trip

---

51. Howell, *Ethnography*, 233–34.

52. Borthwick, "Worth It?" 128.

53. Smith, "Missiological Questions," 45–46.

54. Smith, "Missiological Questions," 53–54.

participants realize and accept that the STM process is far bigger than just an overseas trip, their willingness to participate in post-trip training will likely increase.

In order to better understand the role and need of post-trip training, it can be helpful to understand how STM participants tend to grow or benefit from their trip. Enoch Wan and Geoffrey Hartt present a number of ways that STM participants can benefit from their trip experience:

- Change in worldview
- New attitude toward missions
- New vision for church planting
- New relationships
- Positive perspective on long-term mission commitment
- Foster increased interest in Bible study
- Assessment for suitability for long-term mission work
- Encouragement
- Encourage engagement in compassion and justice ministries at home
- Increased understanding of God's calling on their lives
- Increased understanding of the long-term missionaries' lives and challenges
- Strengthened desire to see ends of the world reached[55]

These are all great benefits, but there is a primary observation to note. Each of these refers to interest, understanding, desire, vision, perspective, or encouragement. This appears to support Seth Barnes's view that STM participants are often the primary beneficiaries of STM work.[56] According to Kurt Ver Beek, it would be a mistake to expect or assume that these things will naturally lead to action and life change over time.[57] Laurie Occhipinti shares a similar view that while many STM participants may feel as though they have been transformed through the trip, the reality is that much of that transformation is not sustained.[58]

55. Wan and Hartt, "Complementary," 97.
56. Barnes, "Changing Face," 108.
57. Ver Beek, "Sapling," 476.
58. Occhipinti, *Globalized World*, 2.

It can be a real challenge for STM trip leaders to move participant thinking beyond casual observations to deep processing of the "why" and "how" of what they are experiencing. Apart from this processing, leading people to radical responses and long-term commitment is very difficult.[59] Zehner encourages trip leaders to get teams back together a few weeks after the trip to further reflect and dialogue through their experience.[60]

In a refreshing shift from the norm, Cuellar makes an argument for the idea that North American churches do not need to decide between either local missions or foreign missions. Instead, the two should be integrated. The Church should be obedient to joining God's mission everywhere in the world whether it be local or global.[61] Cuellar goes on to raise the concern that Christians are willing to spend large amounts of money and effort to go accomplish some level of good overseas while ignoring incredible needs in communities at home.[62] Both points by Cuellar are great and should both be considered with balance. The comments about needing a greater focus at home should not be taken to mean the global should be sacrificed for the sake of the local, but that when both the local and global are emphasized, both benefit. A stronger focus on local mission cultivates the ground for greater openness to global mission. This is true for both STM and LTM, but STM is likely favored since it involves dramatically less commitment. A church with a strong local mission outreach is better equipped to service ongoing, international STM partnerships that are better suited for raising up a generation more open to LTM work. Not everyone is called to LTM work overseas, but everyone is called to LTM work of some kind, somewhere. This model helps foster that.

There is a different kind of follow-up training to consider as well. Thanks to the internet, ongoing connection and training via telephone or internet is now possible. For business professionals or others who served on STM in a training sense, in some cases follow-up with internationals can be done through virtual means or even future trips.[63]

Michael Wilder and Shane Parker attempt to capture the STM process as something with lasting discipleship impact for students. They offer several suggestions that can help support this ongoing process. The first is to

59. Slimbach, "Mindful Missioner," 163–64.

60. Zehner, "Rhetoric," 201.

61. Cuellar, "Bigger Than You Think," 283.

62. Cuellar, "Bigger Than You Think," 284–85.

63. Russell, "Missional Business," 363.

surround students going on STM with relationships that will help the discipleship process.[64] Second, they suggest the need for some kind of ongoing process in the church that would lead student STM participants toward a more missional lifestyle post-trip.[65] The third suggestion is for students to somehow become engaged cross-culturally after they have returned from their STM trip.[66] Lastly, it is suggested that students receive help post-trip to figure out how to assess the impact of the trip and how best to move forward in light of it.[67]

I found many books that offer suggestions on what types of things could be helpful for STM participants post-trip, but very few offer tangible direction and many appear to treat it as an after-thought. Brian Heerwagen talks briefly about the need to live differently, invest in the mission field, guard your mind, hide God's word in your heart, and taking risks. In addition, he mentions engaging in evangelism, finding a ministry, and adopting a people as activities that can help maintain momentum post-trip.[68] David Livermore does a nice job of addressing cultural intelligence and its importance for fruitful STM trips and projects, but does not focus on post-trip development.[69]

I have often heard many people say that STM trips bring about lasting and significant change in the lives of participants. Sometimes I have even heard it spoken of as the primary benefit of STM. If this benefit is used as primary defense of STM, it is an idea worth testing. Ver Beek has found in his research that North American participants in the STM trips he studied saw very little lasting change in their lives or the lives of those they served. Ver Beek went on to analyze thirteen other quantitative studies measuring changes in the lives of participants. Of those studies, eleven of the thirteen found little or no significant life change for participants. This is not to say STM is a vain endeavor. In general, research demonstrates lasting positive change can happen, but it requires the right ingredients of accountability

---

64. Wilder and Parker, *Transformission*, 176.

65. Wilder and Parker, *Transformission*, 190.

66. Wilder and Parker, *Transformission*, 210.

67. Wilder and Parker, *Transformission*, 222–23.

68. Heerwagen and Grudda, *Next Mile*, 77–88.

69. Livermore, *Eyes Wide Open*.

and encouragement.[70] Friesen agrees with Ver Beek and supports the importance and great need for better follow-up and post-trip discipleship.[71]

Ver Beek surveyed 162 participants in STM trips to Honduras to offer relief work after a hurricane. Of the 162 participants, 127 responded. It is important to note that this was not an evangelistic trip or a training trip. Those surveyed were asked to rate how daily actions such as prayer, volunteer time, giving, and interest in outreach were impacted. Around 16 percent reported significant impact, 45 percent a slight positive impact, and 40 percent said there was no change. According to Ver Beek, these findings were similar to most of the other studies he analyzed regarding participant self-perception.[72]

However, when these self-perceptions were compared to real life, the results revealed a different story. For example, 60 percent of respondents said their level of giving to the sending organization increased significantly or somewhat. According to the organization records, 75 percent of them had not given any money and only 6 percent even showed an increase in giving. In this example, it appears that perception and reality were not very closely aligned. If this was true for giving, it is a reasonable conclusion to think it is also true in other areas of perceived growth.[73] This is supported by Friesen who found that in many cases, STM participants not only failed to see positive growth but actually saw regression in key areas of their spiritual lives.[74]

Two of the thirteen studies analyzed by Ver Beek showed significant positive change in the lives of STM participants. Ver Beek found that every qualitative study he found came to the conclusion that STM participants experience significant positive change. In contrast, the quantitative studies heavily lean toward no significant change. It seems that either the studies are wrong or participant perception of change is much higher than reality. Ver Beek concludes that participants did have a very positive experience and intended for that experience to translate into action and lasting change, but in most cases it did not.[75]

---

70. Ver Beek, "Sapling," 476.

71. Friesen, "Long-Term Impact," 183–84.

72. Ver Beek, "Sapling," 479.

73. Ver Beek, "Sapling," 479–80.

74. Friesen, "Long-Term Impact," 183.

75. Ver Beek, "Sapling," 487–89.

Ver Beek goes on to compare life change from STM to life change in the rest of life; the reality is that life change is hard. STM leaders should not be surprised when a week-long experience does not automatically lead to significant change. According to Ver Beek, two factors in particular are key to bringing lasting and positive change in people's lives; encouragement and accountability. Researchers have found that people who have regular accountability for reaching specific goals are much more likely to achieve those goals. Likelihood of achieving goals increases even more if goals are public, specific, and demanding within reason. These results are not affected by whether goals are set by themselves or by others. The same is true for encouragement, which helps provide the motivation to do things you would likely not do on your own.[76]

In summary, Ver Beek concludes that for people to experience lasting change, they need a structure that will provide accountability and encouragement to STM participants before and particularly after the trip for an extended period of time. Ultimately, it is the long-term excellent relationships formed through STM that will contribute most to creating lasting positive change. Structures to help promote this positive growth would likely benefit from things such as written goals shared with the group, accountability pairs, mentors, newsletters, and meetings where they can receive the needed accountability and encouragement.[77] It could be said that preparation and follow-up are actually just as important as the trip itself.[78]

Ver Beek's work is the only chapter of a 22 chapter, popular, edited book on world missions that focuses on long-term growth of trip participants. I say this to highlight how much of an after-thought the subject appears to be. Ver Beek does not simply raise the concern, but he analyzes it and comes to powerful findings and conclusions as evidenced above. The idea that STM is a success regardless of what happens overseas because either way the trip participant is changed for the better appears to be a false presumption. This is a powerful blow to casual and unexamined STM practices.

According to Richardson, if there are no follow-up structures, there will be no behavioral changes in STM participants. Therefore, specific goals and a support structure need to be established.[79] Wilder and Parker have

---

76. Ver Beek, "Sapling," 491–93.
77. Ver Beek, "Sapling," 493–94.
78. Marston, *Seeking*, 188–89.
79. Richardson, "Impact," 553.

found that for lasting transformation to take place in STM participants, they must be part of a structured approach that puts them in environments and situations that force them to process and deal with their experiences.[80] The lessons of an STM trip are not able to be absorbed in the short time that makes up the trip itself. Time for reflection and evaluation after the trip is over in order to fully grasp the significance of the experience is very important. The trip leader's role in being willing to lead and allow participants to question, discover, reflect, and challenge presuppositions and experiences is crucial in facilitating this growth. Multiple opportunities for debrief spread out over a period of time are also a necessity that cannot be overstated.[81]

In summary, some best practices for post-trip follow-up training presented in the literature include:

- Clear follow-up structure and process
- Ongoing accountability
- Ongoing encouragement
- Intentional reflection and evaluation of trip experience
- Community dialogue with focus on action and life-change

CHAPTER SUMMARY

As a result of this literature review, it seems the strengths of STM literature is in the areas of how to prepare a team for a fruitful STM trip. The major gaps left are in regard to creating a mutually beneficial relationship between the STM participant and the nationals they serve and how to promote long-term growth in participants once the trip is over. The pre-trip and trip portions of STM receive the dominance of the attention, leaving very little for the post-trip.

The STM literature reviewed had little to add regarding the long-term impact that is had on trip participants or on the nationals they go to serve. Some helpful material was found regarding the forming of mutually beneficial relationships. Several authors gave attention to the reality of mutual brokenness and therefore mutual need on the part of both groups.

---

80. Wilder and Parker, *Transformission*, 153–54.
81. Blomberg, "Whatever," 606–8.

Emphasis on learning culture and advancing with a humble heart are indirect references to seeking mutual benefit, even though these were not consistent themes throughout the reviewed literature.

It seems one of the greatest faults in the literature is the lack of vision. STM missions do not have to be short-term in mindset, mission, or vision. Just because the length of the trip is short, does not mean the focus or vision for STM also has to be short. If the entire focus is truly on just the trip, then it is difficult to see the value. As I mentioned in the opening, there are plenty of cases in mature STM programs that integrate STM well into a LTM work overseas. Unfortunately, there is little attention given to the long-term growth of trip participants and even less attention on how to facilitate that long-term growth. A significant gap in the literature exists in the area of training STM participants post-trip for long-term missional growth. There are also gaps in regard to how to build mutually beneficial relationships between STM participants and those they go to serve. These gaps are not as glaring as the lack of post-trip training, but are present nonetheless.

In the next chapter, I will review literature on a theory of adult education methodology. My goal is to better understand what adult transformation can look like. With a strong understanding of adult education theory, I hope to be able to better evaluate STM processes and make recommendations that fill some of the gaps found in the literature I have presented here.

Chapter 2

Transformative Learning Theory

I AM RESEARCHING THE idea of STM as an opportunity for transformative growth for all involved, particularly the trip participants. I will review important literature regarding TLT with the purpose of gaining insight into making STM a better process for life transformation among participants. TLT is an idea that in many ways defines modern day adult education, at least in terms of the literature. In this chapter I present an overview of the theory in order to adapt it to my research findings.

TRANSFORMATIVE LEARNING THEORY DEFINED

Jack Mezirow is generally considered the originator of TLT. He defines transformative learning as a process by which we transform our previously uncritically assimilated assumptions, beliefs, values, and perspectives to make them more inclusive, discriminating, open, emotionally capable of change, and reflective.[1] Patricia Cranton adds that transformative learning is all this but also goes beyond being just a cognitive, rational process.[2] Adult learners are defined as mature, socially responsible individuals who participate in sustained informal or formal activities that lead them to acquire new knowledge, skills, or values; elaborate on existing knowledge, skill, or values; revise their basic beliefs and assumptions; or change the way

1. Mezirow, *Learning as Transformation*, 7–8.
2. Cranton, *Understanding*, 2.

they see some aspect of themselves or the world around them.[3] Transformative learning is about making meaning out of experiences and questioning assumptions based on past experiences.[4]

People create meaning out of experiences. When these experiences are combined, they build worldviews that guide how people see and understand the world around them. People expect the world to work in a certain way, according to the worldview they have constructed from their experiences. When something unexpected happens, people have the choice to reject what happens or question their pre-existing expectation. When people seize this opportunity to critically examine and revise existing thinking, then act on the revised thinking, transformative learning then takes place.[5]

TLT was initially described as a process of personal perspective transformation made up of ten phases:

1. Experiencing a disorienting dilemma

2. Undergoing self-examination

3. Conducting a critical assessment of internalized assumptions and feeling a sense of alienation from traditional social expectations

4. Relating discontent to the similar experiences of others—recognizing that the problem is shared

5. Exploring options for new ways of acting

6. Building competence and self-confidence in new roles

7. Planning a course of action

8. Acquiring the knowledge and skills for implementing a new course of action

9. Trying out new roles and assessing them

10. Reintegrating into society with the new perspective[6]

The theory basically breaks down to the idea of encountering some level of disorienting experience that challenges current thinking and leads to new behavior. In the present focus of study, the STM serves as an ideal case of a disorienting dilemma. As Wan found in his research on diasporas,

3. Cranton, *Understanding*, 2.
4. Cranton, *Understanding*, 8.
5. Cranton, *Understanding*, 19.
6. Mezirow, *Learning as Transformation*, 22.

people experiencing the disorienting dilemma of major cultural transition are more receptive to new ideas as a result of the associated disorientation.[7]

Formal TLT is built on the idea that meaning[8] is seen to exist within ourselves, not from the outside. People develop or construct personal meaning from their experience and validate it through interaction and communication with others. Cranton elaborates on this more by saying that if there were absolute truths in the world, the goal of learning would be to discover right answers whether they reflect on individual perspectives.[9]

Learning happens when someone encounters an alternative perspective and prior ways of thinking are called into question. This is what Mezirow calls the "disorienting dilemma."[10] Mezirow goes on to name six kinds of meaning perspectives: epistemic, sociolinguistic, psychological, moral-ethical, philosophical, and aesthetic.

1. Epistemic—Has to do with knowledge, how people acquire and use it.

2. Sociolinguistic—Has to do with social norms, cultural expectations, and how people use language.

3. Psychological—Has to do with how people see themselves, including their self-concept, needs, inhibitions, anxieties, and fears.

4. Moral-ethical—Has to do with how people define good and evil, how they live that out, and how responsible they see themselves for advocating for justice in the world.

5. Philosophical—Often based on a transcendental worldview, philosophy, or religious doctrine, which forms a web of values, beliefs, and rules for living.

---

7. Wan, *Diaspora*, 132.

8. Conceptually, meaning here refers to the construction of meaning within a network of ideas that reflect experience.

9. Cranton, *Understanding*, 23. Cranton appears to paint a black and white picture of extremes that does not need to be the case. In a sense, she seems to be unknowingly lost on the theological quandary of rectifying the existence of a sovereign God and human volition. Without discussing this issue at length, I will say that I believe that TLT and absolute truth do not need to be mutually exclusive of each other. TLT necessitates an imperfect person in need of growth in a world full of choices. While absolute truth is very real, attaining that truth in one's life is often a very undefined process. I see TLT as a means of gaining understanding of how to move forward from where you are. Even though I believe in absolute truth, I do not know where I will find myself in the future or how to get there. TLT helps me grow toward that future.

10. Mezirow, *Learning as Transformation*, 22.

6. Aesthetic—Has to do with people's values, attitudes, tastes, judgments, and standards regarding beauty.[11]

Of these six meaning perspectives, the psychological, philosophical, and aesthetic have the greatest connection to STM. The psychological has great relevance to STM: how people see themselves is typically a primary impact of significant cross-cultural experience. The philosophical also has major cross-cultural relevance for STM. Few people are able to go to the developing world and not question the level of material wealth that people live at in the U.S. The aesthetic can be difficult to distinguish from the philosophical on some levels. Both deal with values, but the aesthetic focuses more on the expression of the values whereas the philosophical more on the inner meaning and belief.

People's worldviews are the product of their knowledge about the world. This knowledge includes their cultural background, language, psychological nature, moral and ethical values, religious or philosophical doctrines, and the way people see things aesthetically. All these go into shaping habits of mind, which remain unexamined apart from a disorienting dilemma.[12] Patricia King and Karen Kitchener created a seven stage model for, what they call "reflective judgment" that can help understand how someone progresses from unexamined habits of mind to continual evaluation of one's world:

1. Beliefs need no justification; what is believed is true.

2. Knowledge is absolutely certain but may not be immediately available.

3. Knowledge is absolutely certain or temporarily uncertain.

4. Knowledge is idiosyncratic; some information may be in error or lost, therefore one cannot know with certainty.

5. Knowledge is conceptual and subjective; it is available through interpretation.

6. Knowledge is constructed by each person and is based on the evaluation of evidence and argument.

7. Knowledge is the product of rational inquiry, which is fallible.[13]

---

11. Mezirow, *Learning as Transformation*, 17.

12. Cranton, *Understanding*, 28.

13. King and Kitchener, *Judgment*, 14–16.

Personal reflection is a key concept in TLT. In essence, reflective thinking is the goal of adult education.[14] Cranton identifies three main areas of reflection:

1. Content reflection examines the content or description of a problem. Includes questions such as, "What is happening here?" "What is the problem?"

2. Process reflection is an examination of the problem-solving strategies that are being used. Includes questions such as, "How did this come to be?"

3. Premise reflection questions the problem itself. Includes questions such as, "Why do I care about this in the first place?" "What difference does this make?" "Why is this a problem anyway?"[15]

Of these three, premise reflection has the greatest potential to lead people to the transformation of a habit of mind.[16]

Transformative learning is the process by which people examine problematic frames of reference to make them more inclusive, discriminating, open, reflective, and emotionally able to change. This process can be triggered by a disorienting dilemma, or gradually and cumulatively over time. Either way, discourse, critical reflection, and critical self-reflection are central to the process.[17] This process is not an accidental or automatic one. Both the learner and the educator have important roles to play in order to maximize the growth opportunity. I will address these roles as well as go deeper into many practical dynamics that can help in applying the transformative learning process to STM.

Role of the Learner

Stephen Brookfield identifies five phases of critical thinking on the part of learners:

1. An unexpected event leads to discomfort or perplexity.

---

14. Cranton, *Understanding*, 33.
15. Cranton, *Understanding*, 34–35.
16. Cranton, *Understanding*, 35.
17. Cranton, *Understanding*, 36–38.

2. Appraisal or self-examination follows in which the event is identified and clarified.

3. During an exploratory phase, the person tries to explain discrepancies found in the appraisal phase and investigates new ways of thinking or behaving.

4. The person develops alternative perspectives in order to try out the new ways of thinking or acting.

5. If the previous phase leads to new perspectives, the individual then integrates the new ways of seeing things into his or her life.[18]

These five phases have a lot of resemblance to Mezirow's ten phases of personal transformation.[19] Both lists follow the basic pattern of disorienting dilemma, evaluation, new thinking and action. Brookfield's phases are less specific and precise and can therefore be reduced into five phases instead of ten. This is a benefit in terms of simplicity but also limiting by not offering as much detail. The benefit of two lists like this is that an STM leader could start with Brookfield's list and then move on to Mezirow's when more detail is desired.

A goal and condition of TLT is learner empowerment. An empowered learner is someone able to fully and freely engage in critical reflection, participate in discourse, and act on revised perspectives.[20] Mezirow sees the act or process of creating the conditions for transformative learning, including critical reflection and discourse, as being the essence of adult education and the defining characteristic of the role of the adult educator.[21] The biggest issue is not the freedom to engage in critical reflection, but creating the space to ensure that it happens. This leads to the role of the educator.

Role of the Educator

It is important for the teacher or educator to exercise authority and power responsibly in order to best facilitate the empowerment of the learner. This is not an attempt to remove the power distance between teacher and learner, but to highlight the importance of using it responsibly. Some suggestions:

18. Brookfield, *Critical*, 25–28.
19. Mezirow, *Learning as Transformation*, 22.
20. Cranton, *Understanding*, 59.
21. Mezirow, "Transformative," 58–63.

- Reduce the trappings of formal authority such as standing in front of the group and using a title.

- Avoid being in the position of providing all of the answers, having the right answers, making all the decisions, and controlling everything that learners do.

- Ensure that access to resources is easily available.

- Lessen the disempowering effect of grading by using some combination of strategies such as learning contracts, self-evaluation, peer evaluation, and flexible learning projects.

- Involve students in controlling the learning environment—both the physical arrangement of the room and the group norms and activities.

- Remain open and explicit about all strategies; learners should know what the educator is doing and why.

- Acknowledge and use expertise as a source of power that builds credibility and trust and serves as a foundation for helping learners question assumptions.

- Develop open and authentic connections with students in which respect and loyalty are meaningful components of the power relations.[22]

Many of the suggestions made by Cranton are focused on a classroom setting, which is not the setting of an STM. Even so, with STM trips there is a clear leader and then a team, therefore the empowerment of the learner is still very applicable. This is where the STM leader benefits by taking a new level of intentionality by choosing to lead the trip not just with the impact stated purpose of the trip in mind, but with the goal of seeing true transformation in the lives of participants. This way the STM has a dual purpose.

In the end, an educator can do nothing to ensure that transformative learning takes place; learners must decide to undergo the process themselves. It is the responsibility of the educator to help people articulate and examine beliefs and assumptions that have been previously assimilated without questioning.[23] Fortunately, there are many things within the power of the educator that can be done.

Some guidelines for asking good questions:

- Be specific—relate questions to specific events and situations.

22. Cranton, *Understanding*, 122–23.
23. Cranton, *Understanding*, 135.

- Move from the particular to the general.

- Be conversational.

- Avoid echoing students' responses to a question.

- Use follow-up questions or probes to encourage more specific responses.

- Do not ask questions that can be responded to in a simple, yes-no way.

- Ask questions that draw on a learners' experiences and interests in relation to the topic.[24]

These are all questions and ideas that can be helpful throughout the STM process, whether on the go or during team gatherings. In order to help them get the most out of the education, learners need to be challenged and given the opportunity to process experiences well. Cranton is correct, you cannot force someone to learn, but you can foster a learning environment and that is an important role of the STM leader with the goal of long-term transformational learning.

Dialogue Education

The purpose of dialogue education is to create optimal learning with adults. Jane Vella identifies six key concepts that help inform the essence of dialogue education:

1. Relatedness—Everything teachers do in design and education is related. All of the twelve steps are related to each other.

2. A holistic perspective—The whole is greater than the sum of the parts and learners learn more than the teachers teach.

3. Duality—Embrace opposites, use both/and thinking, and use open questions that invite both/and thinking and dialogue.

4. Uncertainty—Every theory is constantly being constructed by application to new contexts.

5. Participation—The observer is part of what they observe. Each person's perception of any given reality is different depending on his or her context and culture. People evoke the world they perceive.

24. Cranton, *Understanding*, 138–39.

6. Energy—Learning demands energy. Many of the principles and practices of dialogue education are designed to raise and sustain the energy of learners.[25]

Every one of these six concepts relates one of the primary themes in TLT, the idea of a disorienting dilemma that leads to life change. Duality and uncertainty are designed to shake-up existing assumptions and views so they can be reprocessed and challenged in dialogue and praxis. The STM leader can truly create impactful STM trips by working to become an architect of learning experiences. By designing a trip and training experience that integrates Vella's principles for effective adult learning the STM leader creates a situation where greater impact can be made both near and long-term, both internationally and at home.

CREATING SIGNIFICANT LEARNING EXPERIENCES

Having discussed the theory and idea of transformative learning, then discussed Vella's principles, it is now time to get into the details of what creating learning experiences can look like practically. Table 1 provides a comparison between traditional teaching models and current understanding of what optimal adult education looks like.

Table 1: Old and New Paradigms for Teaching[26]

	Old Paradigm	New Paradigm
Knowledge	Transferred from faculty to students	Jointly constructed by students and faculty
Student	Passive vessel to be filled by faculty's knowledge	Active constructor, discoverer, transformer of knowledge
Mode of learning	Memorizing	Relating
Faculty Purpose	Classify and sort students	Develop students' competencies and talents

25. Vella, *Learning to Listen*, 30–32.

26. Campbell and Smith, *Paradigms*, 275–76.

	Old Paradigm	New Paradigm
Student growth and goals	Students strive to complete requirements, achieve certification within a discipline	Students strive to focus on continual lifelong learning within a broader system
Relationships	Impersonal relationship among students and between faculty and students	Personal relationship among students and between faculty and students
Context	Competitive, individualistic	Cooperative learning in classroom and cooperative teams among faculty
Climate	Conformity, cultural uniformity	Diversity and personal esteem; cultural diversity and commonality
Power	Faculty holds and exercises power, authority, and control	Students are empowered; power is shared among students and between students and faculty
Assessment	Norm-referenced (that is, grading on the curve); typically use multiple choice items; student rating of instruction at end of course	Criterion-referenced (that is, grading to predefined standards); typically use performances and portfolios; continual assessment of instruction
Ways of knowing	Logical-scientific	Narrative
Epistemology	Reductionist; facts and memorization	Constructivist; inquiry and invention
Technology use	Drill and practice; textbook substitute; chalk-and-talk substitute	Problem solving, communication, collaboration, information access, expression
Teaching assumption	Any expert can teach	Teaching is complex and requires considerable training

Several of these concepts are repeating ideas already well addressed by both Cranton and Vella in this paper. Notable exceptions are student growth and goals, relationships, context, climate, ways of knowing, epistemology, technology use, and teaching assumption. The student growth and goals concept has not been very developed up to this point. It does relate to the idea of the empowerment of the learner, but should not be assumed. The difference is not to teach a learner in the moment but empower them to learn for a lifetime. An important aspect of this is setting expectations for the learner that a goal of the course is to continue self-directed learning beyond the course.

The relationship between teacher and learner has already been discussed but Table 1 adds an extra element, the idea of the relationship being personal. This may have been implied by other authors but has not been expressly mentioned. Whenever a relationship becomes personal, the amount of time and energy involved increases notably. Typically, the opportunity for growth and impact increases as well. Like all other elements of transformative learning, this puts more pressure and responsibility not only on the teacher, but the learner as well.

The context of cooperation is another concept that is not entirely new but expressed more specifically than before. Context here is more of a description of relationships than physical environment. The primary factor added in here is the emphasis on student and faculty learning together as opposed to directional from teacher to student. Climate is closely matched with context as diversity is valued over simple conformity. Unity amidst the diversity is important to support the safe learning environment and helps promote a greater variety of perspectives and balance to dialogue.

The ways of knowing concept from the chart adds the idea of narrative as opposed to a logic focus. This different focus allows for greater flexibility, which tends to fit the world around us better than idealized logic and outlines. Narrative is more friendly to gray issues and questions and tends to be much more relatable as well. The new look at epistemology reinforces questioning and interacting with ideas more than simple memorization of facts. The different focus regarding technology highlighting problem solving and collaboration continues along the same line emphasizing the value of narrative ways of knowing. The change regarding teaching assumptions is especially significant. When teaching is more than transferring data, the requirements for who can actually teach change significantly.

CHAPTER SUMMARY

TLT has the potential to be a significant frame through which to view and structure the STM process as a transformative learning experience. A key aspect that links TLT with STM is the idea of the disorienting dilemma. One of the great contributions STM can offer a trip participant in terms of growth is a very disorienting experience that can be capitalized for life change. TLT could serve as a great tool for crafting a post-trip training process that helps participants build on that disorienting experience.

Having completed a review of literature for STM and TLT, I will now turn focus to field research. In Part 2 of this paper, I will share my research findings regarding the practices and benefits of STM. Combined with my review of the literature, my field research will help create a reliable picture of STM that I can use as a basis to build on later in the paper.

Part II

Field Research

IN MY FIELD RESEARCH I address all three phases of an STM process: pre-trip, trip, and post-trip. The focus of my research is finding what was beneficial for both STM participants and the nationals they go to serve. My goal is to find out what needs to be done to create mutually beneficial relationships and how to operate an STM trip in a way that leads to long-term missional development and change on the part of trip participants.

Chapter 3

Methodology, Data Collection, and Analysis

IN THIS CHAPTER I will focus on the methodology, data collection, and data analysis. I will review the various methods used in my research in detail. As for the data, I will discuss my methods of collection and the analysis that followed.

RESEARCH METHODOLOGY

I used several methods to obtain my data. The primary method was unstructured interviews of American short termers and South Sudanese residents who serve as hosts. As secondary methods, I used participant observation and two surveys, which I chose to distinguish as open-ended and closed-ended even though they are very closely related.[1] Even though participant observation is a secondary method, I will report it first throughout my findings so it can serve as a basis for guiding my research and questions. Fortunately, God was gracious in all the phases of my research and I was able to obtain useful data through my interviewing methods, both surveys, as well as my own participant observation along the way. All methods have full human subject research approval. Before beginning my discussion of

---

1. Bernard, *Anthropology*, 211–12. I distinguish these because many of the open-ended survey questions were identical or very similar to the unstructured interview questions, with the primary difference that the open-ended survey questions were given on an electronic fill-in-the-blank interview sheet as opposed to in a live interview setting.

methodology, I want to take a moment to provide some brief background on the nation of South Sudan. The goal of this section is not to give a comprehensive background, but simply enough to provide the reader with some context since the STM trips in my research all take place in South Sudan.

South Sudan Background

South Sudan is my country of focus in my role at Small Organization A where I serve as church planter. All of my STM research participants travelled on STM to South Sudan. In this section, I will briefly look into South Sudan's past and present to help give a better understanding of the context that much of the ministry researched can be found in.

Most of Sudan, and now South Sudan's modern history has been marked by suffering and war. From 1955 to 1972, then 1983 to 2005, the country was wrecked by civil war.[2] In July of 2011, South Sudan received its independence by popular vote. In December of 2013, civil war broke out again, this time it was not north against south, but an internal civil war in South Sudan. Through all of these decades of fighting, South Sudan and its people are deeply accustomed to death and suffering. The country is among the least developed in all of Africa. In 2006, there were a total of six miles of paved road in an area the size of Texas. Running water and electricity are non-existent. Concrete structures are rare and found only in town centers. To have a building for the church to meet in is considered a great luxury. There is very little economy, most people provide for themselves through subsistence farming on a family garden. Meals consist of a few staple items; meat is a great luxury. In the midst of this, there is much joy and community mixed with notable suffering and hardship.

The church has a rich history in South Sudan in the modern era. For centuries, missionaries have tried to reach this land with the gospel and some have had varied success. It seems that South Sudan has largely been a mystery to Westerners and the best means by which to reach them with the gospel has been elusive. Ironically, radical Islam has been both one of the greatest persecutors and greatest strengtheners of the church in South Sudan. As radical Islam tried to force itself upon the southerners it was Christianity that they turned to for their identity and as a unifying factor. Undoubtedly for many their allegiance to Christianity was as much a stand against Islam as it was a stand for Christianity. Nonetheless during

2. Johnson, *Root Causes.*

the times of greatest struggles it was Christianity that served as the rallying point and place of refuge and strength amidst great suffering.[3]

This background information is significant for my study because it presents a very brief picture of what life in South Sudan is like. For Americans travelling on STM, many for the first time, to a culture so radically different from their own it can be expected there will be a high level of disorienting dilemma that takes place. With this in mind, I turn attention back to research methodology.

Primary Methods

I selected one primary method, unstructured interviews, to serve as the foundation of my research. There are also three secondary methods that I will discuss in the following sections with the exception of participant observation. While it is a secondary method, participant observation served as a basis of observation that informed my question formation throughout the interview and survey process. These methods were meant to supplement the primary method and help account for any issues with validity that may exist.

Participant Observation

Data that can be gathered through interviews and surveys can be immensely valuable but alone will always fall short of telling the full story. Unfortunately, the researcher can never know the entire story, but by entering into the worlds being researched researchers can greatly expand the data collected as well as enhance their ability to analyze that data.[4] As mentioned, the unstructured interviews are my primary means of data collection, the open-ended surveys, and closed-ended surveys helped reinforce the interviews while participant observation provided a lot of filling and context that I could never access apart from my own participation in what I was studying. Participant observation also contributed greatly to the development of my interview guides. Thanks to my experiences, I was better able to ask relevant questions to interviewees.

3. Werner et al., *Devastation*.
4. Bernard, *Anthropology*, 342.

Participant observation allowed me to enter more closely into the world of the subject. In doing so, I could make my own observations, speak from my own experience, take my own photos and notes.[5] In this way, the opportunity was presented to collect all kinds of data, often that I would never have thought to pursue otherwise. Utilizing participant observation protects against subjects changing behavior or responses because they are being studied.[6] Even more so, participant observation meant more than simply observing but also actually participating.[7] The aspect of participation was especially significant when studying relationships like I did for this research.[8] This participation helped me when listening to subject interviews and responses to have a context to understand them more fully. I was also able to formulate better questions since I already had data to work with from my personal observations.

A downside of participant observation was that it could lead to me to becoming biased. There was the potential that I would be tempted to discount or disregard certain data obtained as opposed to receiving it with fresh eyes and ears. I could have become lazy and missed details and could have been tempted to disagree and cast judgment on data given and the subjects providing it. To account for these I made it a point to remind myself of these dangers throughout the research process.

Unstructured interviews

The primary method I used is the unstructured interview.[9] I interviewed each of my subjects once and made sure there was a relaxed feeling and freedom to discuss things that may not be covered in the questions, but I also made it a point to insure that the time was used well. For this reason, I had the questions in front of me to keep the interview on track. My primary interview subjects were Americans who have traveled with me to South Sudan on a STM trip. I, or a co-worker, also interviewed South Sudanese pastors who have worked with Americans on STM trips.

All subjects were asked the same set of questions in the same order, but the set of questions was different for the Americans (Appendix A) and the

5. Jorgensen, *Participant*, 23.
6. Bernard, *Anthropology*, 354.
7. Spradley, *Participant Observation*, 51.
8. Jorgensen, *Participant*, 12.
9. Bernard, *Anthropology*, 212.

South Sudanese (Appendix B). The two sets of questions were very similar, but there were variations because some questions asked of the Americans were not relevant to the South Sudanese. The subjects were allowed to answer however they liked and the interviewer was encouraged to follow-up questions where necessary to emphasize points or clarify any confusion. All subjects had the consent form explained to them and agreed to its terms in advance.

I chose to use the unstructured interview because I believed I would gain a higher quality data by speaking to people individually in a dialogue format.[10] Ethnography aims to learn from people rather than simply study them and the unstructured interview was a great method for that.[11] The primary information I sought for my research was the subject's perspective on whether or not they formed mutually beneficial relationships, what helped or possibly hurt that process, and what the results of those relationships were regarding long-term missional engagement by participants. There are complex issues that would be difficult or impossible to properly understand through methods such as survey, but interview opens the door to more complex questions and data collecting.[12] The strengths of interviewing were that they allowed me to interact with subjects firsthand in a situation where we were both active and collaborative in the data collection process.[13] This allowed subjects to elaborate on points and speak to blind spots that I had overlooked when designing the interview. Interviews also allowed me to pursue points made by subjects to a deeper level and to take note of other aspects of communication such as tone, body language, mannerism, etc.

The primary weakness of unstructured interview is that it is time intensive and therefore limiting as to number of subjects who can participate and how many can be interviewed due to time limitations. I could only conduct a limited number of interviews whereas I could potentially send out hundreds of surveys. I compensated this weakness by also using open-ended surveys, closed-ended surveys, and participant observation that all worked to potentially affirm or contradict data gathered through interview. Another weakness of interview is the risk of the interviewer somehow biasing the subject. Through the questions that are asked and the way the

10. Spradley, *Ethnographic*, 58.

11. Spradley, *Ethnographic*, 3.

12. Rubin and Rubin, *Qualitative*, 2–4.

13. Holstein and Gubrium, *Active Interview*, 4.

interview is conducted the way the subject responds to the questions could potentially be impacted.[14] As I interviewed, I saw this happen at times. For example, due to my pre-existing knowledge of the situation, at times I was tempted to avoid asking certain questions that could have been uncomfortable. There was even a few times where I skipped a question fully out of human error. To help with these concerns, I sought to create a positive rapport with the subject and make my goals and intentions clear so they could be more comfortable and have a context for understanding the intent of my questions.[15] Another weakness worthy of note is the fact that transcribing interviews is a very time consuming process.

Secondary Methods

I selected three secondary methods to help supplement the unstructured interviews. Each method has its own strengths and weaknesses and my hope was that together they could complement each other enough to provide more reliable data that I could use with confidence in forming my conclusions. The three secondary methods were the participant observation (see "Primary Methods"), open-ended survey, and closed-ended survey.

Open–Ended Survey

I wanted to conduct open-ended surveys as a means of gathering more data to supplement the unstructured interviews. I created an interview sheet (Appendix C) with comment boxes and emailed it to the Small Organization A director and a missions pastor at Large Church B who together emailed it to a total of 440 subjects who had travelled to South Sudan on an STM trip with these two organizations. I used self-administered questionnaires conducted through the Internet, specifically the website *Survey Monkey*.[16] The questions were very similar to those used in the unstructured interviews. The open-ended survey questions were given as part of one questionnaire that also included the closed-ended survey questions.

One strength of the open-ended survey is that it can reach many more people than the unstructured interview. It was no more work for me to

14. Holstein and Gubrium, *Active Interview*, 8.
15. Spradley, *Ethnographic*, 58–60.
16. www.surveymonkey.com.

send the survey questions to 440 people than it was to send it to four. This is able to produce a much larger set of data to work with. With this larger set of data, I could then compare it to my core set of data gained from my unstructured interviews and look for confirming or contradicting data. Another strength is that the subject types all of the responses, which eliminates any need for transcription on my part.

The weaknesses of the open-ended survey is the dark side of one of its strengths, it can produce a lot of data! It can be very time consuming and overwhelming to code and sort through this quantity of data. In the end, time limitations did prevent me from being able to code the data from my open-ended survey results as well as I would have liked. Unstructured interview also does not allow for follow-up to gain a better understanding of what is meant by a particular reply. There is no chance to try to gain more clarity for answers that do not initially make sense when read on their own.

Closed–Ended Survey

The main purpose of the closed-ended survey was to gather basic feedback from people I was not able to reach through interview due to time and logistical limitations. I did not use closed-ended survey as a primary means of collecting data, therefore I did not have the same concerns regarding sample size that would normally impact a survey. I used self-administered questionnaires conducted through the Internet, specifically the website *Survey Monkey*. These surveys were a helpful supplement to the interviews, unstructured and structured, and participant observation.

The closed-ended surveys allowed me to gather data from a large number of people I would have otherwise been unable to reach due to time and other restrictions. The potential to gather data from a much larger pool than I could through interviews helped me gain a much broader perspective that helped to either affirm or contradict data gained through the other methods. The anonymity of closed-ended survey can also provide a means for people to share thoughts in a safer, more private environment. Self-administered surveys such as these are also easy to conduct and all subjects respond to the same questions with little room for bias.[17] Specific to my research, closed-ended survey helped me to acquire data from subjects who were six months or more removed from their STM and helped give a better

17. Bernard, *Anthropology*, 258.

answer to whether there was lasting change in their life resulting from the STM trip.

The weakness of closed-ended survey is the limitations on depth and variation. The data received is limited to the questions that are asked and there is no room to explore uniqueness in responses or follow-up data with more questions. These gaps were hopefully made up for in my research by the other, more primary methods of unstructured interviews, open-ended survey, and participant observation. Another weakness is the possibility of confusion or misinterpretation caused by the closed-ended survey questions that you have no means to clarify. There is also the possibility that someone will complete the closed-ended survey, other than the intended recipient, but this risk seems very small regarding my research.[18]

Limitations

I am based in the U.S. and therefore my knowledge and research of the impact on South Sudanese is limited to the limited time I am with them. Similarly, my understanding of the impact of STM on individual lives and contexts is limited in most cases to what they verbally share with me since I am unable to observe them all regularly. To overcome these limitations, I interviewed a total of nine South Sudanese pastors and workers from three different parts of the country. This allowed for a more varied data set. While I do live in the U.S., I have been working in South Sudan since 2007. During that time I have learned much about the South Sudanese people. This knowledge also helped me to overcome these limitations.

DATA COLLECTION

In this section I will look at the actual details of the data collection process for each of my research methods. I will first share my thoughts from my participant observation. Then, I will move on to my primary and other secondary methods.

---

18. Bernard, *Anthropology*, 260. All of the surveys were sent to personal email addresses and there was no incentive for someone to take a survey in place of someone else.

Participant Observation

I have personally been involved in STM trips since 2002 and have been leading teams of students since 2003. In this time, I have spent a summer in East Asia, three summers in Central Asia,[19] and some time in Slovakia all with Cru.[20] I have been traveling to South Sudan on STM since 2007 and began leading teams there this year (2012). During this time, I travelled to South Sudan alone in the summer of 2007 where I met up with an existing team and I did the same in 2009. I also spent two months in Ethiopia with a team from Serving in Mission (SIM). I was the team leader for all three of the teams that I interviewed. This means that I was with all of the Americans who participated in an unstructured interview, throughout their pre-trip training, the trip itself, and corresponding follow-up. This gives me the opportunity to gain a lot of insight into the STM process in South Sudan. The pre-training lasts approximately three months, the trip lasts nine days, and the follow-up is on-going.

Procedure of Collecting

The extensive time with the subjects throughout the above mentioned process allowed me the opportunity to make observations, take notes, conduct informal interviews through conversations, make observations through photography, and provide me a strong foundation through which to gather and analyze the data that is collected through the other methods.

Beyond these, I have been working to build mutually beneficial relationships with South Sudanese myself through active participation.[21] During my trip in September of 2012, I lived with one of my South Sudanese partners in his home, with his family. We used the same facilities and ate the same food. In my second trip in October and November I labored beside my South Sudanese counterparts in the work of the gospel. We dreamed together, prayed together, planned together, and served together. Through activities such as these, I had a truly great opportunity to participate as well as observe. Throughout each of these trips and activities, I kept a log of

---

19. I led two of these trips that consisted of college students.
20. At the time known as "Campus Crusade for Christ."
21. Spradley, *Participant Observation*, 60.

observations and feelings as part of my data collection process to be ana-lyzed later.[22]

Nature of Data

The nature of the data consists of my memory and notes from all of the trips mentioned above and surrounding activity. In this paper, the data will show up as in text format as my observations and interpretations of my personal experience. This data will be very helpful in filling in gaps as well as provid-ing a more full picture of how relationships are formed, things that serve as catalysts and the training before and after that effects the process.

Reliability of Data

The reliability of the data has the strength of being a first-hand account from someone with extensive experience but is limited in that it is still only one account. It is impossible for one person to observe and capture ev-erything and equally impossible to not allow bias to impact the collection and analysis process. For these reasons, participant observation is only one method that is being employed and it is a secondary method at that.

Unstructured Interviews

The primary focus of my research was the long-term impact of these STM trips on Americans, but the long-term impact on South Sudanese is just as significant for the overall mission of Small Organization A. The data gained from the South Sudanese has been crucial to my research as it helps provide a better understanding of how mutually beneficial the relationships are formed and the extent of their impact. In total, I collected data from 18 interviews; nine Americans and nine South Sudanese. The audio of all interviews was recorded and later transcribed.

Procedure of Collecting

The interviews of Americans averaged between 20 and 40 minutes depend-ing on how talkative the subject was. There were five teams that were primary

22. Spradley, *Participant Observation*, 58.

in my study: the team from my trips in March, October, and November of 2012, and two different teams from two different local churches, Large Church A and Large Church B, traveling to South Sudan in October and December of 2012 respectively. All together this provided approximately 37 potential interviews of Americans. In the end, I interviewed nine Americans, all from the teams that I led in October and November of 2012 and felt that the data was consistent enough to not warrant more interviews.[23] I obtained permission from Small Organization A, Large Church A, and Large Church B to interview and survey people in their organizations. I also acquired consent from every person that participated in unstructured interviews (Appendix D).

I personally performed all of the American interviews, in Dallas, Texas from late December 2012 through January 2013. One of the nine American subjects was a pastor and two others were in seminary training for ministry. The remaining six subjects were all laypeople. The subjects had a variety of mission's experience ranging from the South Sudan trip being their first STM trip to spending up to two years overseas. Most of the subjects had been on a few week-long STM trips in addition to our trip together to South Sudan.

Each interview of an American was done in person at least one month after the subjects returned from South Sudan. The longest period between return from South Sudan and the interview was close to ten months, but most averaged between one-to-two months between their return from South Sudan and the interview. All American subjects interviewed were males; there were two females who travelled with me to South Sudan and were eligible for the research but neither was available to be interviewed.[24]

For the South Sudanese interviews, I personally performed four in Kajo Keji, South Sudan in September 2012 and a fifth in November of 2012, also in Kajo Keji. Due to logistical limitations regarding time and distance I was unable to interview more pastors in person, but two of my coworkers were able to interview four more South Sudanese pastors in person in South Sudan all in November of 2012, one in Nimule, South Sudan and three in the Kala Valley region of South Sudan. The range of experience working with American STM stretched from as much as ten years to as little as one, with most falling somewhere in the middle. All interviews were done in English with no translator with exception of the one in Nimule, which was

23. Gibbs, *Analyzing*, 91.

24. This was purely the result of timing and availability.

done in English through a translator. The interview lengths for the South Sudanese ranged from 14 to 26 minutes. The length of the interviews was largely influenced by my desire to focus on a limited set of information as well as on language limitations.

Each interview of the South Sudanese was done in person throughout South Sudan. Each South Sudanese pastor interviewed had widely varying levels of experience in working with Americans. All of the pastors were male, but this was not the intention of the study. The primary reason for the lack of females is because the large majority of workers are males and these are the people who have the most exposure to Americans and therefore a greater relevance to this study.[25]

Nature of Data

All of the data collected through interviews in this study is qualitative but in some cases can be organized and quantified with numbers. For example, in some cases when several subjects give a similar response, I have given the response and list the number of subjects that shared that view. This allowed me to compare the popularity of particular answers. For each category of data that I collected, I have listed the responses in order of the frequency that they were mentioned with the number of mentions next to the response in parenthesis. In most situations, responses occurring once or twice were not listed. Even so, those responses may be reflected in my observations that follow if they add value.

Following each ranked list of responses are my observations on the data. I began to interpret the data that was presented and help understand how it fits into the bigger picture message that the data is revealing. I saved specific application and ramifications of the data for summary and conclusion sections to follow.

Reliability of Data

The reliability of the data is reinforced by the fact that there are nine separate accounts by both the Americans and South Sudanese for a total of eighteen interviews. This number of interviews can lead to corroboration or reveal noteworthy discrepancies. Everyone from each set was asked the

25. There are a few female workers that could qualify for this research, but I have not been able to interview them as of yet.

same questions to create consistency and to help with making comparisons between responses from separate subjects. Each interview was also conducted independently of the others, which protects from collusion or an inhibition of originality. This way any discrepancies would indicate genuine disagreement that could warrant further research. The presence of the open-ended surveys and surveys were intended to support and reinforce the findings of the unstructured interviews.

One possible concern with reliability would be the language gap for the South Sudanese interviews, which were all conducted in English, a second language for them. While English is a second language for each of the South Sudanese subjects, several of the subjects speak very good English and the data from these interviews can serve to provide helpful reinforcement, contradiction, and ultimate clarity to the interviews from those with weaker English.

Open-Ended and Closed-Ended Surveys

Open-ended and closed-ended surveys served as secondary research methods in support of the primary method of unstructured interviews.

Procedure of Collecting

I sent a combined open-ended and closed-ended survey online to all individuals who have travelled to South Sudan with the organizations Small Organization A and Large Church B in Dallas Suburb, Texas. I did not personally send the surveys, but gave the information to a leader in each organization to send to their relevant constituents. This proved to be somewhat limiting as I was unable send reminder or follow-up emails to help produce a greater completion return rate. There were emails sent to 265 people from Small Organization A and 175 from Large Church B with a link to the survey for a total of 440 potential participants. The surveys were sent out in late January 2013. I waited until late January because I wanted to be able to make adjustments to the questions after I had a better grasp on the type of data that I had already received from the unstructured interviews. In the end, I received back 58 completed open-ended and closed-ended surveys giving a competed return rate of 13.2 percent (see Appendix A and B).

Nature of Data

The open-ended survey data is in the form of text given in comment boxes as answers to the questions on the open-ended survey questionnaire. I will present this data in Chapter 4. I will consider and speak to the qualitative contribution of the data and in some cases present the data in quantitative statistics to provide extra clarity when relevant to do so. The closed-ended survey data will be presented in charts in this paper that show the question, responses by percentage and the overall number of responses for each answer. I will then give my observations and interpretations on what the answers communicate and the overall value contributed to the research.

The overall role of the surveys is to supplement the unstructured interviews and look for how the data produced either reinforces or contradicts the primary data of the unstructured interviews. In addition, the data from the surveys provides an overall larger pool of data that can provide a much greater confidence in my findings. These "extra" interviews also allowed me to get data from subjects who went on STM trips to South Sudan with leaders other than me and even another organization.

Reliability of Data

The reliability of the data is strengthened by the fact that there are 58 completed interviews representing responses from two different organizations and many different leaders. The data was provided voluntarily and anonymously so that subjects had no incentive to be untruthful in their responses. This data is also one piece of a much larger set of data contained in this paper so there is a lot of room for comparison and testing of reliability.

DATA ANALYSIS

In this section, I will address the actual process of data analysis. My actual findings are not presented here.

Analytical Procedures

I transcribed all audio recordings from the interviews and uploaded them into the online program "Dedoose."[26] Dedoose allowed me to code my data consistently and most importantly provided a very simple and fast means for looking for code co-concurrences that helped me to see how different codes related to each other. I developed my codes both inductively and deductively. Apart from the data coded by question, as I studied the data I looked for key points that I determined should serve as codes and began to create my code tree in this manner. Over time, a clear list of definitions (codes) began to develop. Once I completed the coding, I used Dedoose to analyze all of the unstructured interviews according to interview questions as a form of preliminary analysis (see Appendix A and B). I then did the same thing according to each research question and then according to the nine primary codes (see "Relevant Codes").

Relevant Codes

In addition to themes, I chose to code my data according to its interview question number and according to which research question it related to. This proved to be very helpful when it came to organizing my data. While I ended up using a total of 179 codes, 58 were codes relating to coding by question, 112 were second and third level codes that helped with specificity and organization, and ultimately nine proved to be the primary codes that helped me grasp the meaning of my data. The nine primary codes were:

1. Gold—Used to highlight something of notable value
2. Unique—Something with questionable value but was unique among the other responses
3. Pre-Training—Anything leading up to a trip
4. Post-Training—Anything following up a trip
5. Helpful for relationships—Anything that helped create relationship
6. Obstacles to catalyst—Anything that obstructed potential growth or benefit

---

26. www.dedoose.com.

7. Result of Relationship/Catalyst—Any results of the relationships or specific catalysts

8. Types of catalyst—Something that served as a catalyst for growth or benefit

9. Unhelpful/Missing for relationships—Things that obstructed relationship or were missing and needed

Supporting Theory

I utilized grounded theory as I inductively collected and analyzed data in my qualitative research.[27] It was my intention that theory and data would be an ongoing conversation throughout the research process. I believe that the data should have room to speak for itself and not be restricted to the theories and presuppositions that I bring to it.[28] Specific to anthropology I primarily operated from a postmodern theoretical approach.[29] I tried to enable as many voices to speak into and through this research. I gathered and interpreted data to find out what the data means and what is behind the data. In a departure from postmodern theory, I do believe that while there is uniqueness in all cultures and peoples, there is still great commonality in being formed in the image of God. The primary methods I used to gather this data have been discussed fully above and are: unstructured interview, open-ended survey, closed-ended survey, and participant observation.

SUMMARY

In Chapter 3 I focused on research methodology and my overall approach to my field research. For each of my research methods, I discussed the procedure of collection along with the nature and reliability of the data. Then, analytical procedures, coding, and supporting theory were discussed. In Chapter 4, I spend time sharing and analyzing my actual findings. These findings, when combined with my review of the literature form the basis for my change recommendations in Part III.

27. Gibbs, *Analyzing*, 149.

28. Charmaz, "Grounded," 335.

29. Barrett, *Theory and Method*, 150–55.

Chapter 4

Data Findings

IN THIS CHAPTER, I reveal my findings based upon the research described in Chapter 3. Findings are laid out chronologically in sections based upon their flow in the STM process: pre-trip, trip, post-trip. As mentioned, participant observation is presented first among my methods due to the role it served as a basis for my initial observations and the formation of question guides for the interviews and surveys. Even so, it is still a secondary method to the unstructured interview.

PRE-TRIP

This section on pre-trip training and preparation relates back to how STM trips currently operate. The issue of pre-training, for the sake of this study, only pertains to Americans so all data contained in this section is from the American subjects. The primary theme that arises from the pre-trip data is that participants really want training and preparation for their trips. This comes out in the unstructured interviews, both surveys, and is also verified by my personal observations. Trip participants want to be ready for their ministry roles, they want to know what to expect, and many of them want more training than they are currently receiving.

Participant Observation

I have had pretty good experience with pre-trip preparation from personal experience. I have also lead one trip to South Sudan with very little pre-trip preparation and two more with several months of preparation. The more people can be prepared for what to expect and how to handle situations, the more confident they will be going into the trip and they will usually have a better experience on the trip. Tables 2 and 3 reinforce the idea that trip participants highly value this kind of preparation.

On the trip that had very little preparation, every member of the team had problems with evangelism to some degree because they do not evangelize much in the U.S. and were unprepared to do so in South Sudan. The other two trips that had more preparation were better prepared with how to approach evangelism, but still expressed a need for more time practicing sharing their faith. We struggled to make time to actually practice evangelism during our meetings or preparation even though I planned to do so on numerous occasions. The problem we ran into was logistics continued to consume all of our meeting time. Again, an underlying theme seen here is that almost all focus is entirely on the trip alone.

Unstructured Interview

I will first look at what participants found helpful and unhelpful in the pre-trip training they received. I begin with what characteristics were found to be helpful as seen in Table 2. The numbers reflect how many times each theme was mentioned; one individual could mention a category more than once.

There are three primary things that the subjects especially appreciated and want: preparation for culture, ministry, and logistics. I am encouraged to see that prayer was mentioned four times. Note that all the training focus is on the trip itself and little thought is given to the personal transformation of the participants. I will now turn attention to Table 3 which captures responses about what was lacking or unhelpful in pre-trip training.

Table 2: Helpful in Pre-Trip Training

Helpful Characteristics	# of Mentions
Cultural and historical background	11
Creation to Christ evangelism training	5
Prayer	4
Trip logistics and planning	4
Presence of experienced team members	3
When Helping Hurts book	2
T4T book	2
Building relationships with teammates	2
Total Respondents =	9

The primary thing, by far, the subjects wanted more of was training in evangelism. Each of the subjects was given materials but actual time together as a team was not spent practicing the material and this is clearly an area that needs to be addressed. As with the areas of training the subjects appreciated above, here we see all four of these areas that were lacking falling into preparation regarding culture, ministry, or logistics. These results also highlight how equipped participants feel for the work of evangelism and how great of an opportunity STM trips are to equip the saints in this way.

Table 3: Lacking or Unhelpful in Pre-Trip Training

Lacking Characteristics	# of Mentions
Practicing Creation to Christ story for evangelism	9
More training in how to connect cross-culturally	4
Better awareness regarding the difficulties of the trip	3
More culture and history training	2
Total Respondents =	9

Closed-Ended Survey and Open-Ended survey

The closed-ended surveys and open-ended surveys were conducted at the same time with Americans who had travelled on STM trips. The two are combined because many of the open-ended survey questions correspond to the survey responses. Remember, the idea is to assess how well the pre-trip training prepared participants for STM work.

Surprisingly almost one quarter of subjects did not feel as though they received any preparation that helped them form better relationships with the South Sudanese. Of those that answered "yes," when asked what was helpful, subjects primarily referred to training they received on culture and history with limited mention of ministry specific training. Many mentioned the significance of spending time with teams that had previously gone on a STM trip to South Sudan similar to the trip they were going on as a significant help.

Table 4: Preparation for Forming Relationships

Did you receive preparation for the trip that helped you form better relationships with South Sudanese?		
Answer Options	**Response Percent**	**Response Count**
Yes	77.2 percent	44
No	22.8 percent	13

Some of the Americans also mentioned how helpful discussions on trip logistics and planning was in advance. I believe this was because the more concerns and distractions that can be removed from the Americans, the more they are able to focus on the task at hand and getting to know the South Sudanese. In the end, the primary training that helped with building relationships was cultural and historical background that helped the subjects to more easily focus on getting to know the people rather than the context and place.

Table 5: Missing Training for Relationships

Was there training that you would have liked to have received but did not?		
Answer Options	**Response Percent**	**Response Count**
Yes	31.6 percent	18
No	68.4 percent	39

As indicated in Table 5, most subjects feel they were adequately prepared. Those who mentioned things they believed were missing brought up a variety of things. The more prominent were the desire for more culture and history background as well as some language training, even though they acknowledged that would be very difficult. Some mentioned a desire for more ministry training regarding the work they would be doing on the trip.

Open-Ended survey

American subjects were asked what was helpful in their preparation as well as what was unhelpful or missing. A variety of things were mentioned that reinforced findings from open-ended surveys. Subjects found time with STM trip veterans to South Sudan very helpful, time in prayer and fasting, evangelism training, and general preparation regarding logistics and expectations. It seems that many people are getting helpful preparation for their STM. The primary forum for this preparation was team meetings leading up to the trip that also provided another important benefit, the chance for the team to get to know each other before the trip.

An overwhelming number of subjects responded that nothing was missing from their trip preparation. Those who did say something was missing mentioned things such as help with building relationships with South Sudanese, interaction with the South Sudanese they would be working with in advance of the trip, how to preach a sermon, and more on culture and language. These responses correspond well to and reinforce much of what was found in the unstructured interviews.

Summary

As mentioned at the beginning of the section, the theme that participants really want training and preparation for their trips comes through evidentially. Participants placed a very high value on the training for ministry and relationships that they received. To add to this, Tables 3 and 5 show that many participants would have liked to receive even more preparation than they already had.

TRIP

This section on the STM trip focuses on how STM trips currently operate and how STM participants are shaped by the STM experience. This section is broken down into two major sections: cross-cultural relationships and catalysts for growth. Both American and South Sudanese responses are considered.

Cross-Cultural Relationships

In the following section, I examine the cross-cultural relationships formed between both the South Sudanese and the American participants. The relationships are examined using interview, survey, and participant observation. Themes that surfaced from the data are summarized at the end of the section.

Participant Observation

In my experience, building relationships in South Sudan on STM is not dramatically different than building relationships with Americans here at home. Some of the most significant dynamics are time together and shared experience. When I played football in high school, friendships were formed with guys from all different racial and economic backgrounds. These friendships were a function of a few factors:

1. Being united around a common cause

2. Lots of time together (structured and unstructured)

3. Shared struggle

I have seen these three factors to be true of STM. Americans and South Sudanese both benefit by understanding the big picture vision of why they are doing what they are doing. Likewise, they benefit by understanding very clearly how their specific STM fits into that vision and what the end goal for the specific trip is. These goals are challenging and give the Americans and South Sudanese something to strive for together. I have also seen the benefits of having boundaries in place for when the time for work begins and ends each day. This way everyone can know when the work is finished for the day and have time to celebrate the day and all that was accomplished by relaxing and playing together.

In the end, time is the significant factor and one STM trip of a week or less is not enough to build a lasting friendship, but when an STM trip is followed up by ongoing correspondence and successive trips I have seen strong relationships begin to be formed. My relationship with my church planting partner Dominic is a great example. In the past year, I have spent time with him during four STM trips over the past year and have kept in regular contact via telephone. It has taken time, but I can tell that a corner has been turned as of the most recent trip and the correspondence that has followed. With each trip, more trust is built and comfort level increases between us. Something else that has helped during this time is that we are coming closer and closer to sharing a common and clear vision for the work we are partnering in.

Another significant dynamic for building relationships is comfort. The higher level of comfort someone can have in a particular context, the better equipped they are to form relationships and thrive in that environment. I remember my first trip to South Sudan in June 2007 and how nervous I was. This impacted my experience and ability to relate and minister to people. Contrast that to my experience fall of 2012 when I travelled to South Sudan on my own, was with only South Sudanese the entire time, and felt very comfortable and at home. In this context, I was able to relax and have a richer experience, including better time with the South Sudanese. This reinforces the importance of preparing teams as well as possible regarding trip logistics and expectations that will help the trip participants to feel more at ease and comfortable with the new environment. Things as simple as daily schedules, routines, and help with basic things like how people will brush their teeth and take showers. All of these things are stresses that can be greatly relieved through preparation and expectations. Lastly, time is a significant component to building this kind of comfort. Not necessarily extended individual periods of time but returning and staying involved over a period of years. This kind of enduring involvement brings a familiarity that can provide experiences like the one I had last fall that allowed me to spend an entire trip with just South Sudanese and thrive while doing so.

American and South Sudanese Combined Responses

In this section, I show the combined results of the American and South Sudanese unstructured interviews. The most helpful things for building relationships between Americans and South Sudanese, according to all subjects, are found below in Table 6.

Table 6: Helpful for Building Relationships (Combined)

#	Helpful Characteristics	# of Mentions	South Sudanese	American
1	Serving together	21	15	6
2	Serving the same God	13	12	1
3	Down time together	12	4	8
4	Equality in Partnership	12	12	0
5	Praying together	8	7	1
6	Encouragement	7	7	0
7	Showing genuine interest in each other	7	5	2
8	Concentrated relationship	6	3	3
9	Eating meals together	6	2	4
10	Humility	6	6	0
11	Learning attitude	6	2	4
12	Long-term involvement	6	5	1
13	Playing together	5	0	5
	Total Respondents =	18		

Items 1, 3, 5, 9, 12, and 13 all relate in various ways to having time. For each of these items, the focus is not on attitude, personality, training, or experience, but simply on being together and doing things together. The key takeaway is simply the importance of being together.

Items 4, 6, 7, 8, 10, and 11 all relate to the people's attitude and person specific traits. While the previously mentioned items focused on being together, these items focus on the quality and nature of that time together. This is significant because it reveals that there is more to these relationships than just being together and sharing experiences, but the nature of that time is also important. Item 2 stands in a class on its own as it directly relates to the common bond and unity that both Americans and South Sudanese share in the Body of Christ.

When asked what things were lacking or served as obstacles to forming relationships the following responses found in Table 7 were given.

Table 7: Things Lacking and Obstacles in Relationship Building (Combined)

Deficiencies	# of Mentions	South Sudanese	American
Language difference	6	5	1
Lack of time	4	1	3
Inequality in partnership	4	4	0
Cultural difference	3	2	1
Total Respondents =	*18*		

The first thing to note is that there are dramatically fewer items that were noted as missing or an obstacle as compared to the list of items that where helpful for relationships. This tells me that there are a lot more things going right than there are wrong. While each of these four items was mentioned, not one of them was cited as a major issue that could not be navigated with minimal work. From my personal experience, I can attest that language is the biggest deterrent, but by no means an insurmountable one. The primary way that language shows through as an issue is that it slows the ability to develop deeper relationships because deeper conversation is more difficult. In my experience, time does a lot to overcome this. In just one year of regular trips and phone calls I have seen my relationship with my South Sudanese church planting partner grow significantly.

American Responses

The most helpful things for Americans when building relationships with South Sudanese, according to the American subjects, in order of times mentioned can be found in Table 8.

Table 8: Helpful for Building Relationships (American)

Helpful Characteristics	# of Mentions
Down time together	8
Serving together	6
Playing together	5
Eating meals together	4
Learning culture from South Sudanese	4
Concentrated time together	3

Helpful Characteristics	# of Mentions
Total Respondents =	9

All six of the most helpful things mentioned by American subjects relate directly to the kind of time together or how the time was spent. Specifics about the nature or attitude of the South Sudanese or Americans are not mentioned as a factor. I wonder whether this is a reflection that the Americans view the time with the South Sudanese as a ministry or service and therefore they see the time a sacrifice in which they are not expecting something in return from the South Sudanese. Possibly, the South Sudanese are so easy to work with that it is taken for granted and specifics regarding how this contributed to the relationships did not seem worth mentioning by the American subjects.

The fact that serving together and playing together were outranked by down time together is very interesting. This seems to communicate that while serving together was significant, the real value when it came to building relationships came during relaxed and less structured settings. These settings typically allowed for more opportunity to have conversation and learn more about each other as opposed to the time serving together, which is typically very focused time that is also physically, and emotionally draining.

Things that were lacking when building relationships with South Sudanese, according to the American subjects, in order of times mentioned can be found in Table 9.

Table 9: Lacking for Building Relationships (American)

Lacking Characteristics	# of Mentions
Lack of time	3
Cultural differences	1
Language Difference	1
Community not prepped	1
Warm-up time with translator before serving	1
Total Respondents =	9

There are very few things mentioned here, particularly compared to the list of things that are helpful. A primary problem that I would have expected is a lack of time, but still only three subjects out of nine mentioned this. The comment on the community being prepped was a suggestion that the time in the community doing evangelism could be more fruitful and potentially easier to build relationships if the community was prepared in advance to receive us and spend time together. The warm-up time was a suggestion that before going out to serve together each day it would be helpful to have some time to talk and spend time with the South Sudanese translators to build camaraderie before stepping out and serving together. It should be noted that none of these issues were mentioned as major issues but more as suggestions that were given when prompted by question.

Closed-ended surveys and open-ended surveys were conducted at the same time with Americans who had travelled on STM trips. The two are partially combined here because many of the open-ended survey questions correspond to the closed-ended survey responses.

Table 10: Relational Benefit to Americans

Were the relationships you formed with South Sudanese beneficial[1] to you?		
Answer Options	**Response Percent**	**Response Count**
Yes	98.2 percent	56
No	1.8 percent	1

The results found in Table 10 are an affirming and very clear response. Overwhelmingly the American subjects considered their relationships with the South Sudanese to be beneficial to them. The one subject who said "no," judging from his other responses appears to have taken the question in a very matter of fact manner and felt that he did not experience a significant benefit from his relationships with the South Sudanese as I can see no evidence of anger or spite in his responses. The same subject answered a later question affirming that he did think the relationships formed with the South Sudanese were beneficial. Either way, it is clear that most of the American subjects clearly felt they benefited from the relationships with the South Sudanese.

When asked how the relationships were beneficial to the Americans a variety of answers were given, but three clear themes developed among them: challenged, encouraged, and new perspective. Some subjects were challenged to see things differently, others to live differently. Many subjects

---

1. The term "beneficial" was left intentionally vague because the I wanted to see if trip participants perceived their relationships with South Sudanese beneficial, in any way.

were encouraged in their faith and speak of a bigger picture of God and their role in serving Him. Very few subjects mentioned any kind of tangible benefit from the relationships. Instead, almost all of the answers seemed more related to the intangible benefits of being challenged, encouraged, and gaining a new perspective but it is uncertain from this question alone what, if any, lasting impact came from this.

Table 11: Relational Benefit to South Sudanese

Do you believe the relationships you formed were beneficial to the South Sudanese?[2]		
Answer Options	**Response Percent**	**Response Count**
Yes	91.1 percent	51
No	8.9 percent	5

A few more subjects questioned whether the relationships benefited the South Sudanese, but the sentiment was still overwhelmingly of the impression that the South Sudanese benefited from the relationships. When asked how they believe the South Sudanese benefited, "encouragement" was repeatedly given above and beyond any other response. Several subjects shared that the time was too short for significant benefit and the general lack of tangible benefits mentioned could indirectly reinforce this idea that there was not enough time to impart or realize lasting change. Perhaps they were there long enough to be a catalyst for change, but not there long enough to witness the impact. Subjects did mention a variety of tangible benefits that should not be ignored such as South Sudanese that came to faith in Christ, ministry training that took place, physical needs that were met, prayer, and in some cases relationships began that are still active today through email and successive STM trips.

The question in Table 12 is simply a reinforcement of the previous two and a way to get clearer and more consistent picture of how the subjects perceived their relationships. In the case of the subject who answered "no" to the relationships being beneficial to him, this question proved helpful in getting a better picture of what he thinks. The American subjects strongly believe that the relationships they formed were beneficial both to

2. This question is very subjective, but important because it helps gauge the perceptions of trip participants. If the trip participants perceived their time with the South Sudanese was not beneficial to the South Sudanese that could reveal opportunities for further research.

the Americans and the South Sudanese. There was not a corresponding open-ended survey question for this survey question but the responses that have been given and discussed above provide a backdrop for understanding how the American subjects perceive these relationships as being mutually beneficial.

Table 12: Mutuality of Benefit

Do you believe the relationships you formed with South Sudanese were mutually beneficial?[3]		
Answer Options	**Response Percent**	**Response Count**
Yes	91.1 percent	51
No	8.9 percent	5

Table 13: Obstacles to Mutual Benefit

Were there things that interfered with the building of mutually beneficial relationships between you and the South Sudanese?		
Answer Options	**Response Percent**	**Response Count**
Yes	53.6 percent	30
No	46.4 percent	26

The majority of the 53.6 percent (30 subjects total) of subjects that said there were obstacles, 12 mentioned language and 10 mentioned time as the major interferences with building mutually beneficial relationships. Three of those who mentioned language as a problem also mentioned time creating a small overlap, meaning that a total of 19 different people out of 56 subjects responding mentioned either time or language as an issue. This means that 67 percent of the subjects saw neither time nor language as barriers to building relationships. Clearly language and time are an issue, but not one that two thirds of subjects saw as significant.

3. Similar to the question posed in Table 11, this question is very subjective. Even so, it is important because it helps gauge the perceptions of trip participants. If the trip participants perceived their time with the South Sudanese was not beneficial to the South Sudanese that could reveal opportunities for further research.

South Sudanese Responses

As a result of unstructured interviews of South Sudanese the items in Table 14 were found helpful for forming relationships with Americans.

Table 14: Helpful for Building Relationships (South Sudanese)

Helpful Characteristics	# of Mentions
Serving together	15
Serving the same God	12
Equality in Partnership	12
Praying together	7
Encouragement by Americans	7
Humility of Americans	6
Long-term involvement by Americans	5
Americans showing genuine interest in knowing the South Sudanese	5
Down time together	4
Americans listening	3
Extended time together	3
Concentrated relationship	3
Total Respondents =	9

A few initial observations are that the South Sudanese have many more responses than the Americans did. There were more questions for the South Sudanese that were directly targeted at forming relationships, which I am sure, is a major reason. There is also no mention of playing together, which was the number two ranking response by the Americans. It is possible that playing together is indirectly referred to through down time together. On that note, down time together does not show up until the ninth spot for the South Sudanese whereas it ranked number one for the Americans. I wonder whether these differences communicate a difference of values when it comes to relationships. It is also possible that things like down time and playing together are assumed aspects of relationship where the Americans see it as an important divergence from what they are used to back home.

The South Sudanese were very impacted by the Americans willingness to join them in the work of the Gospel in South Sudan. This is evident through the focus on equality in partnership, encouragement, humility, listening, and taking genuine interest in the South Sudanese. During the interviews, several South Sudanese commented on how much it meant to them that the Americans left their home full of wealth and comfort to travel so far and join them in their much more humble state of living. Judging by the answers given here, it is very clear that this means a lot to the South Sudanese.

These results also seem to communicate that the South Sudanese have a greater focus on the work and mission than the Americans did, particularly when looking at the amount of attention given to serving together as compared to the Americans where it came in third. The second response by the South Sudanese emphasizing that one of the more helpful things for building relationships is the fact that they serve the same God as the Americans. This appears to be a unifying factor that is mostly taken for granted by the Americans.

Unstructured interviews with South Sudanese found the items in Table 15 to be obstacles or issues with forming relationships with Americans.

Table 15: Obstacles or Issues for Building Relationships (South Sudanese)

Deficiencies	# of Mentions
Language differences	5
Inequality in partnership	4
Cultural difference	2
Judgment of others	1
Total Respondents =	9

Unsurprisingly, language differences are the number one concern for the South Sudanese since the burden is on them to be able to communicate with the Americans in English. Even though they mention language as an obstacle, in each instance they shared that the primary issues came in the beginning with people who were new to South Sudan and that over time the problems faded as they all learned to communicate better with each other. The inequality concerns are also not surprising after seeing how important the South Sudanese considered equality when it came to having good relationships with the Americans. It is worth noting that those who mentioned inequality as an issue shared it in more of a hypothetical concern than one that has actually happened in relation to an STM trip. The judgment issue was only mentioned once but is insightful and interesting. The subject who brought this up shared how other South Sudanese in his community judged him for working with the Americans, claiming he was only doing it so that he could benefit materially. He asserted that his intentions were genuinely to honor the Lord and advance His Kingdom.

Summary

The data clearly supports the themes mentioned at the beginning of the section. Of particular note is how highly both the Americans and South Sudanese valued their time together and saw it as very beneficial. Even more interesting is that while both found this time significant, they valued it very differently. The Americans especially focused on the value of the rest and recreation time together whereas the South Sudanese focused on the time serving together. The data supports that there is a very high level of perceived benefit from the time together between both groups.

Interviews were conducted of both Americans and South Sudanese. I have analyzed the combined findings of the Americans then the South Sudanese. There are a few major themes that stand out from the data regarding the cross-cultural relationships formed between Americans and South Sudanese:

- Time together was the major factor for forming cross-cultural relationships.

- The Americans especially appreciated the down time and recreation time with the South Sudanese for forming relationships.

- The South Sudanese especially appreciated the time together serving with the Americans for forming relationships.

- After time together, attitude was the second major positive factor for forming relationships.

- Language and cultural differences were mentioned as obstacles for relationships, but not major obstacles.

- The South Sudanese especially highlighted the fact that they were all serving the same God as a significant component in forming relationships.

Catalysts for Growth

In the following section, I examine what served as catalysts for growth in both the South Sudanese and the American participants. Catalysts are examined using interview, survey, and participant observation. Themes that surfaced from the data are summarized at the end of the section.

Participant Observation

STM trips have served as a significant catalyst for me over the last eleven years. The most significant catalyst has been the experience in itself. I do not think of individual people or experiences but the overall experience of being on mission for God in a foreign and challenging environment. Another important aspect to this is the reality of the need in overseas missions and the ability the Lord has given me in being able to help with that need. These have been significant catalysts in my life, but most of the follow-up has been reliant upon my own efforts and determination as there was no structure in place to lead me along with what to do and where to go. Praise God for His grace, guidance, and patience.

In my experience, the most significant aspects of long-term growth and change are: (1) A plan, (2) Encouragement and (3) Accountability.[4] I have not had any of these things as a part of my STM trips in the past in any formal or consistent way. Just recently in January 2013, I have begun to have formal follow-up meetings held with the intention of providing this plan, encouragement, and accountability that I believe is so needed. It is still too early to tell what the long-term impact will be, but the initial response has been very positive.

American and South Sudanese Combined Responses

Unstructured interviews were conducted of both Americans and South Sudanese. I will begin by analyzing the overall combined findings followed by the Americans then South Sudanese. Overall, what Americans and South

---

4. Kurt Alan Ver Beek wrote an article on STM where he spoke on lasting positive change and expressed the importance of a structure that provides both encouragement and accountability. This article has had a significant influence on my thinking. Ver Beek, "Sapling," 493.

Sudanese viewed these items as the most significant catalysts for life change can be found in Table 16.

This information is helpful as it gives a picture of how the various catalysts rank with each other overall. Some of the responses can clearly be attributed to either the Americans or the South Sudanese. Items 5 and 6 are notable in that they highlight the importance of on-going relationship of some kind showing that staying connected beyond the scope of the STM trip can be a very significant catalyst in itself.

What Americans and South Sudanese viewed as the primary results of the catalysts for life change in Table 16, can be found in Table 17.

Table 16: Significant Catalysts for Life Change (Combined)

#	Catalysts for life change	# of Mentions	South Sudanese	American
1	Provision of teaching and training resources	11	11	0
2	Providing a model for ministry	10	7	3
3	Influence of Pastor A	10	0	10
4	Passion of South Sudanese/ Americans	9	1	8
5	On-going prayer	8	3	5
6	On-going relationships	8	1	7
7	Evangelism Together	7	4	3
8	Boldness and openness with Gospel	6	1	5
9	Conversations with South Sudanese	6	0	6
	Total Respondents =	18		

Four of the top six overall results of catalysts are intangibles that may or may not lead to on-going life change. As with a pep rally, if there is no lasting follow-up, each of these benefits would likely fade over time with no reinforcement. Responses 3, 5, 7, 9, 10, and 12 are all tangible skills or clear results that have already been impacted and with ongoing practice, have a strong likelihood of lasting life change.

Data Findings

Table 17: Results of Catalysts (Combined)

	Results	# of Mentions	South Sudanese	American
1	Encouragement	30	15	15
2	Perspective	26	2	24
3	Stronger in evangelism	24	15	9
4	Challenged	21	5	16
5	Better equipped for ministry	17	16	1
6	New vision for the future	14	6	8
7	Reaching the unreached	14	14	0
8	Prayer for each other	13	10	3
9	Better church planter	10	9	1
10	Material needs met	10	9	1
11	Validation	7	4	3
12	Better Bible teacher	4	3	1
	Total Respondents =	18		

Americans and South Sudanese shared the obstacles to the catalysts in Table 16 taking affect. The results can be found in Table 18.

Table 18: Obstacles to Catalysts (Combined)

Obstacles	# of Mentions	South Sudanese	American
Callous heart	1	0	1
No long-term vision	1	0	1
Time	1	0	1
Total Respondents =	18		

The first thing to notice is how short and anemic this list is. Then, it should be noted that all three of these responses came from American subjects. I will discuss these more in-depth in the section focusing on American responses below.

American Responses

This section collects the results of the American unstructured interviews. American respondents identified the items in Table 19 as catalysts for life change experienced during their STM to South Sudan.

Table 19: Catalysts for Life Change (American)

Catalysts	# of Mentions
Time with Pastor A	10
Passion and faith of South Sudanese	8
On-going relationships with South Sudanese	7
Conversations with South Sudanese	6
Boldness of South Sudanese with the Gospel	5
On-going prayer for South Sudanese	5
Relationships with the team	3
Total Respondents =	9

The number one catalyst for change for the Americans was time with our South Sudanese director, Pastor A. I had not expected this, but as I worked through the data his name continued to come up and to the degree that he warranted his own code. What this shows is that respondents recognized the value of time with Pastor A. Pastor A is a South Sudanese man who is deeply committed to the Lord whose faith and commitment in the Lord along with his joy for life are very contagious to be around. Most of the Americans that took part in these interviews are young men in their twenties who do not have many strong men of God in their lives on a regular basis. I think in many ways Pastor A was filling a significant, felt void in these young men's lives that they likely did not realize they had. Pastor A has strong English and is very accustomed to spending time with Americans and this makes him the easiest and most natural South Sudanese person to connect with. I would like to see further research on how much of Pastor A's impact on trip participants was based upon him being South Sudanese versus American and how much of it was due to the participants being in the midst of the disorienting dilemma of the trip.

Virtually every catalyst for the Americans is directly tied to relationship with the South Sudanese whether it is their passion, boldness, or just time with them in general. The Americans did not focus on the experiences themselves or the results of the ministry, but the impact that happened as a result of being with and knowing the South Sudanese. The only non-South Sudanese related catalyst was the relationships the team built with each other. It is very rare for Americans to have the chance to be together continuously for over a week with the same people, experiencing new things toward the end of a common, challenging goal. Times like these are rare and serve as powerful times of unity and forging friendships.

American respondents identified the items in Table 20 as results of the catalysts mentioned in Table 19.

Table 20: Results for Catalysts (American)

Results	# of Mentions
Perspective	24
Challenged	16
Encouragement	15
Stronger in evangelism	9
Vision for future	8
Deeper understanding of South Sudanese culture	4
Validation for South Sudanese	3
Total Respondents =	9

Four of the top five results are intangibles that fade without some kind of follow-up and support. The trips were clearly very eye opening for the Americans as nine subjects mentioned a change in perspective 22 times. I often tell people that if they want to know that things are like in South Sudan, imagine things at the 180-degree opposite of what they are in Dallas; these responses seem to affirm this. The Americans were deeply impacted in how they view their lives back in the U.S. once they have seen how radically different life was in South Sudan. The impact was often linked back to the fact that the South Sudanese had so little when it comes to material things, yet so many of them were happy, strong in the Lord, content, and full of joy. As has been mentioned, some of this is the result of being on a short trip and not staying long enough for some of the more difficult realities of their lives to sink in. For example, large-scale problems with alcoholism, death rates, lack of medical care, lack of education, and significant battles with the elements and poverty. It is easy for Americans to come for a week and fail to appreciate how significant these struggles are. Even so, there is still much to be said about the joy and faith that the South Sudanese have amidst struggles like these and I am very happy that the chance to be exposed to the South Sudanese in this manner is having such an impact.

These dynamics of the South Sudanese's lifestyle and faith led to not just a new perspective, but encouragement and challenge to live differently for the Americans. The most tangible takeaway for the Americans is that they felt stronger and more confident in evangelism as a result of the STM trip. Each of these results mentioned are great for creating momentum that, if captured and followed-up well, can lead to significant life change in the Americans.

American respondents identified the items in Table 21 as obstacles to the catalysts from Table 19 taking affect.

Table 21: Obstacles to Catalysts (American)

Obstacles	# of Mentions
American is callous from previous STM	1
American has no long-term vision for how to move forward after STM	1
Total Respondents =	9[5]

According to the American subjects interviewed, it appears that there is not much that serves as an obstacle to the catalysts occurring during the STM trip. The comment about callousness came from a subject who had travelled on several STM trips in the past and was already familiar with what to expect and knew that the past trips had not dramatically changed his life and therefore did not expect it to happen this time either. One person only made this comment, but it is very telling because I believe it represents a lot of people's experiences on STM. The reality for this subject is that he went on STM trips in the past and in the end the impact did not last. The other obstacle mentioned is also a reflection on follow-up. This subject was not able to capitalize on the catalysts in the trip because he had no vision for what that would look like at home in the U.S.

Closed–Ended Survey and Open–Ended Survey

The closed-ended surveys and open-ended surveys were conducted at the same time with Americans who had travelled on STM trips. The two are

---

5. Not all respondents mentioned an obstacle.

combined because many of the open-ended survey questions correspond to the survey responses.

Table 22: Life Change Resulting From Relationship

Is your life different now because of the relationships you formed?		
Answer Options	Response Percent	Response Count
Yes	87.7 percent	50
No	12.3 percent	7

Of the 50 subjects who responded "yes," the primary themes that arose from their responses were: perspective, awareness, and understanding. The perspective largely pertained to their view of life back here in the U.S. whereas the awareness and understanding primarily related to their view of life for the South Sudanese. In that way these ideas are linked. Their view of South Sudanese and their lives is now much better informed and that has led them to view their lives in the U.S. through a different lens. What is largely missing here are tangible ways that subjects' lives have changed. This continues to reinforce my thinking that most STM participants have little to no help and are typically unable to translate their experiences on STM back to their lives in the U.S. in a constructive way. The over 12 percent of subjects who answered this question negatively reinforces the need for follow-up as well. It is my assumption that these people would like to be able to answer this question with a "yes."

Table 23: Lasting Nature of Life Change for Americans

Do you expect these life changes to continue for you?		
Answer Options	Response Percent	Response Count
Yes	98.1 percent	52
No	1.9 percent	1

As the above chart shows, the subjects are very confident that the life changes they mentioned and experienced will continue. Again, while some of the subjects do refer to specific actions they have or plan to take, there seems to be an overall ambiguity as to why they are so confident. I do believe that mindsets will likely never be the same as they were before the trip, but due to the lack of tangible responses it seems that subjects are speaking as much out of hope and optimism as they are reality. In addition, something that is almost completely lacking and very significant from their responses is community or outside help. Virtually all subjects give individual responses of what they independently intend to do or think with no reference to outside help or direction.

Table 24: Lasting Nature of Life Change for South Sudanese

Do you expect these life changes to continue for the South Sudanese?		
Answer Options	Response Percent	Response Count
Yes	88.2 percent	45
No	11.8 percent	6

There were more tangible and encouraging answers given by the South Sudanese than for the Americans as mentioned above. Many subjects referred to the training they provided to the South Sudanese as reasons they thought the changes would endure along with the importance of on-going trips back to follow-up with them and the on-going presence and discipleship of local national leaders. Some subjects mentioned prayer and the fact that this is the work of God and He will finish and complete the good work.

A surprising and encouraging number of subjects gave very specific and tangible responses as to how they are now involved in various church planting or outreach related activities. Some of the subjects were already involved in these ministries, but several mention their involvement as a direct result of the STM trip. There were several answers that mentioned new perspectives and some were honest enough to say that nothing had changed.

Table 25: Impact on Church Planting and Community Development

Has your involvement in church planting or community development here at home changed at all as a result of this trip?		
Answer Options	Response Percent	Response Count
Yes	63.0 percent	34
No	37.0 percent	20

I cannot help but wonder how many more people could give very specific and tangible answers to this question if they had some dedicated follow-up to help them channel what they learned in South Sudan on STM back to their lives in the U.S. In the end, 37 percent of subjects say their lives have not been impacted in a significant way regarding church planting and community development. I see this as a glaring sign that changes need to be made in how STM trips are conducted or STM leaders need to ask what the true intentions are in using trips to begin with.

Open-ended Survey

Subjects were asked what things were most impactful to them about their relationships with South Sudanese as well as the trip as a whole. The far and away most significant point of impact from the relationships with the South Sudanese came in the form of inspiration. Clearly, the time with the South Sudanese served to inspire the American subjects through a variety of ways such as: their joy, dedication, strength, generosity, love for God, humility, kindness, faith, optimism, forgiveness and courage.

Reading through the responses, a few observations stand out to me. For one, it appears that the radically different way and condition of life that the South Sudanese live compared to the Americans on the STM trips is deeply impactful. Realizing the dramatic disparity between the two lifestyles is a major wake-up call. One of the biggest impacts this seems to have is that the Americans realize the South Sudanese possess so many of the coveted characteristics listed above that most Americans strive so hard for, but wealth cannot attain it.

Second, the Americans speak of the South Sudanese in an incredibly idealistic manner. Surely, much of the praise is warranted, but I cannot help but see a correlation to grandparents visiting their grandchildren. The grandparents come visit and are there for a very short period of time and see everything with rose-colored lenses. The visit is not long enough for the glow to wear off. I do not mean to undermine the South Sudanese as I can attest to the wonderful character and attributes of so many of them, but I cannot help but think the Americans going on one STM trip are naïve in their views.

Third, since most of the benefits or impacts mentioned as a result of the relationships are in the form of inspiration with no on-going follow-up, the STM runs the risk of being nothing more than a pep-rally for the Americans that bears little long-term fruit. This is a major failure on the part of STM trips that must be accounted for if churches and para-church organizations are going to continue to lead them with integrity. I have heard so many people say that the primary benefit of Americans going on STM trips is the impact that the trip has on them. I fear that impact is far less significant than many people want to believe.

The question asking subjects what things were most impactful about the trip as a whole offered more broad responses than how they benefited from the relationships with the South Sudanese as a whole but still focused on ways they gained new perspectives or were challenged and encouraged in various ways. Many of the subjects were impacted significantly by an experience of God, serving God, community, and lifestyle so incredibly different than their own, but still great in its own right. These impacts can serve as powerful catalysts for change when they are able to be adapted well back into their lives in the U.S.

South Sudanese Responses

This section collects the results of the South Sudanese unstructured interviews. South Sudanese respondents identified the items in Table 26 as catalysts for life change experienced through their time with the Americans.

Table 26: Catalysts for Life Change (South Sudanese)

Catalysts	# of Mentions
Teaching and training resources	11
Americans providing model for ministry	7
Evangelism together	4
On-going prayer by Americans	3
Discussing strategy and technique	2
Provision of motorbikes	2
Total Respondents =	9

All six of the catalysts mentioned by the South Sudanese relate directly to their ministry. Each one of these is a catalyst that equips and helps them to serve better. The two most commonly given responses of resources and models for ministry are very helpful. The South Sudanese are looking for direction and help in their ministry and do not have many places to turn. Many of them do not know how to move forward in their ministry and both want examples and need training. This is encouraging because these are things that Americans have and are able to help with during STM trips.

South Sudanese respondents identified the items in Table 27 as results of the catalysts mentioned in Table 26.

Four of the top five are results that tangibly impact ministry and the top result is a reflection of how important something as simple as encouragement is. The South Sudanese have placed a very high value on prayer. As I read this, I wonder how many Americans are indeed praying faithfully for the South Sudanese once the trip is over. The South Sudanese do not shy away from making it clear that the material benefits that Americans can bring to the table are indeed significant and appreciated. I was surprised by how many of the subjects said that validation in the eyes of the community was an important result. Several American subjects mentioned this as a way they expected the South Sudanese to benefit and it is affirming to see it be validated here.

Table 27:Results of Catalysts (South Sudanese)

Results	# of Mentions
Better equipped for ministry	16
Encouragement	15
Stronger in evangelism	15
Reaching the unreached	14
Americans praying for South Sudanese	10
Better Church Planter	9
Material needs met	9
New vision for future	6
Challenged by Americans	5
Validation in eyes of community	4
On-going relationship with Americans	4
Better Bible teacher	3
Spiritual reward	3
Total Respondents =	9

I am also encouraged to see that the Americans have challenged the South Sudanese as the Americans have already affirmed the reverse is true. Lastly, the mention of spiritual reward was edifying and challenging to me personally as this is something I rarely take into account, but it was a blessing to have this mentioned three times as an important result of these trips.

South Sudanese respondents identified no obstacles present that interfered with the mentioned catalysts taking affect. I find this encouraging and a reason for thanks. I am glad that the South Sudanese mentioned some negative things elsewhere in the paper. This way, when I see nothing mentioned as in this case, I can have greater confidence that it is not because they are afraid or unwilling to do so.

Summary

Virtually all respondents, American and South Sudanese, viewed their time together as consisting of many catalysts that lead to notable life change. This is very encouraging. It is also insightful what specifically each group found to be a positive catalyst. The Americans were greatly impacted by the faith and practice of the South Sudanese whereas the South Sudanese were most impacted by the training and resources received. It is notable that the strengths of each group so closely aligns with the deficiencies of the other. The data indicates that the time together was perceived universally as very beneficial. The question remains as to how lasting these benefits turn out to be over time.

As I explored the catalysts for life change that occurred in the relationships between the Americans and South Sudanese, the following themes presented themselves.

Primary catalysts for Americans were the inspirational faith and courage of the South Sudanese.

Primary benefits for the Americans were new perspective, encouragement, and having been challenged.

Primary catalysts for the South Sudanese were the training and resources they received from the Americans.

Primary benefits for the South Sudanese were being better equipped for ministry and being encouraged.

For both parties, the strength of one party very well complemented the weakness of the other in a way that appears to be very mutually beneficial.

Each of these themes can be traced and evidenced in the data gained through my interviews, surveys, and personal participant observation.

POST-TRIP

In the following section, I examine the post-trip experience for American participants. The post-trip portion of STM is examined using interview, survey, and participant observation. Themes that surfaced from the data are summarized at the end of the section. The issue of follow-up training, for the sake of this study, only pertains to Americans so all data contained in this section is from the American subjects.

Participant Observation

In the eleven years that I have been working with STM trips, I have not had one trip that has had any follow-up that has extended beyond a one-session debrief time as a team. These times were very helpful, but left me to find my own way afterward. Many of the lessons learned, perspectives gained, and challenges received began to fade along with the relationships I had formed with my teammates. The last two teams that I have taken to South Sudan are now involved with a monthly follow-up meeting that I hold in my home. We have met twice and had a lot of success helping the teams to stay connected to the work they were a part of in South Sudan and also translate what they learned into their lives here in the U.S.

Unstructured Interview

Subjects found the aspects of their post-trip training found in Table 28 as helpful for facilitating long-term missional engagement after returning from the trip.

Four of the top five responses all relate directly to maintaining and transitioning momentum created by the trip. These responses are encouraging, but not surprising. The third response, relating to staying connected to the South Sudanese, was a surprise and encouraging as this is also the number three ranking catalyst for change given by the American respondents. These responses help confirm my view that encouragement and accountability are two of the most significant aspects of long-term growth and very needed in post-trip follow-up.

Table 28: Helpful for Long-Term Missional Engagement

Helpful Characteristics	# of Mentions
Encouragement	11
Accountability	10
On-going connection to South Sudanese	10
Regular meetings	9
General team fellowship	9
Teaching and resources	3
Long-term vision	3
Prayer	2
Total Respondents =	9

Subjects found nothing from their post-trip training to be lacking or unhelpful for facilitating long-term missional engagement after returning from the trip. This is encouraging, but it is also important to note that the data was collected only two months into the follow-up process. It would be good to also keep in mind that most people have no expectations of trip follow-up and therefore are likely to not notice or consider something as lacking.

Closed-Ended Survey and Open-Ended Survey

The closed-ended surveys and open-ended surveys were conducted at the same time with Americans who had travelled on STM trips. The two are combined because many of the open-ended survey questions correspond to the survey responses.

Table 29: Presence of Follow-Up Training

Have you received any follow-up training after the trip?		
Answer Options	Response Percent	Response Count
Yes	26.3 percent	15
No	73.7 percent	42

Over 70 percent of people who went on STM to South Sudan participating in this study said they received no follow-up training. Those who did went on to describe their training as something that consisted of a meeting for the purpose of debriefing and processing the experience. No on-going follow-up training was mentioned. There were mixed views as to how helpful the follow-up was, some appreciated it and some said it was unhelpful or they were not able to even remember. If long-term change in Americans going on STM is a goal, then on-going follow-up and training is a glaring issue that needs to be dealt with.

When asked what was helpful, unhelpful, or missing from follow-up training 26 of the 39 people that responded said they received little or no follow-up training. Many of those who did mention follow-up training referred to a basic "debrief" meeting that gave some pointers for adjusting back home and dealing with culture shock. The few that mentioned helpful follow-up emphasized how they appreciated being able to process the experience by talking with fellow trip participants who could relate and understand.

When asked what was missing from follow-up training, a few valuable points were made. One subject said they would have appreciated more time getting updates on and praying for the South Sudanese they had worked with as opposed to fully focusing on themselves. Another subject said they would have appreciated a greater focus on sharing the gospel here in America as opposed to just discussing how to tell others about their trip.

Summary

Participant data reveals a significant gap in the STM process regarding training once the trip is over. This is especially concerning when considering the benefits participants perceive themselves to have received as seen in Table 20. Without post-trip training to help capture these benefits, there is a high probability that they will not be maintained over time and lead to a lasting transformed life. Some major themes that arose out of the post-trip training portion of the data are:

- Encouragement and accountability are major factors in aiding long-term impact.
- On-going fellowship with teammates and connection to the work in South Sudan were highlighted.
- Ultimately, there is a major gap regarding post-trip training as most subjects received little to no post-trip training.

FINDINGS SUMMARY

The data has been very helpful in better understanding how Americans and South Sudanese benefit from their time together and why. According to the data, the time together is very beneficial for both parties. Questions remain as to the lasting impact of those benefits and how pre- and post-trip training for trip participants could be changed to better promote lasting change in their lives.

Potential Value of Research

This research has the potential to change the way STM trips are done and to transform STM trips into a major catalyst for life change and on-going discipleship for trip participants. At its least, this research will help me to better use STM trips as a catalyst for life change in the lives of those who travel with me. I expect this research to also impact the approach of my co-workers at Small Organization A. In reality, I fear that many people who read this information will likely not put it into practice because in the end, discipleship is slow and even messy at times. Discipleship and long-term growth take a lot of time and work, whereas a single STM trip can be a lot of work, but it is over when the plane lands back in the U.S. My hope is that this research will serve to open the eyes of many to the great opportunity that STM trips can be toward a revival in church planting and community development here at home.

Gaps and Need for More Research

At present, there is the need to study more in-depth how people's lives look different one or more years after an STM with and without follow-up training. I would also like to find other ministries that do support their STM participants with follow-up training and learn from their program and study its processes and results. Another opportunity for research is to interview STM leaders and find out why post-trip training is not done more.

Basic Takeaways

Many specific, tangible takeaways arise based upon the findings above. When it comes to building relationships with South Sudanese, Americans most value shared experiences with down time, play time, and time serving together topping the list. The South Sudanese value serving God together as equal partners in the ministry as the most significant factor for building relationships with the Americans. This seems to communicate to me that both the Americans and the South Sudanese are focused on shared experience when it comes to building relationships. The primary difference appears to be in how they both view that shared experience. The Americans generally seem to be more focused on the recreational aspect of the experience with the South Sudanese being more focused on the serving side of the experience. The extra component on the side of the South Sudanese that is so significant as well is the impact of the Americans treating the South Sudanese with equality. The primary obstacle is language, but it was not expressed as a major issue.

In regard to catalysts, the Americans are most impacted by the South Sudanese themselves. Their faith and passion for the Lord along with their humble lifestyle tends to leave a significant mark on the Americans. This impact effects the way they view and want to live their lives at home in the U.S. The South Sudanese are in general more impacted by the training and resources they receive with the result that they are better equipped for ministry. I find it insightful to see how different the benefits are between each group, but very encouraging to see that there are indeed very significant benefits impacting both Americans and South Sudanese.

When it comes to pre-trip training, the Americans are most concerned with culture, ministry preparation, and general logistics and preparation. The Americans are very eager to know as much as possible in advance of the trip. This desire to know in advance can be verified from my experience as very important in building relationships and experiencing impact on the trip. I believe the reason for this is that the more comfortable someone is, the more present and prepared they will be for forming relationships and experiencing life change.

In regard to post-trip training, there appears to be a significant deficiency. Subjects show a strong need and desire for on-going training that can help them to capitalize on the catalysts from the trip. I have suggested that there be some kind of structure that provides encouragement and accountability is what is most needed.

Chapter 4 presented my research findings and combined with Part 1 of this paper offers much to build on in terms of change suggestions. In Part III of this paper, I will spend time offering my thoughts and suggestions as to what opportunities for change regarding STM exist. Many of these suggestions will be based upon gaps in the STM process revealed by my research, namely the need for great post-trip follow-up.

Part III

Application/Change

HAVING EXPLORED THE LITERATURE and engaged in research both among American STM participants and South Sudanese hosts, I now want to look at how to create a more full STM experience. I believe TLT has much to offer in terms of viewing STM as a course where the trip is an integral component but still one piece of a larger process of life change. In light of the literature review and field research, I would like to re-imagine STM in a way that utilizes TLT toward the end of developing long-term missionaries at home from STM participants.

Chapter 5

Facilitating Learning Experiences

I BELIEVE THAT TLT could be used as an overall framework through which STM leaders can design an entire STM experience from pre-trip to trip to post-trip. The idea of an STM leader designing an entire discipleship course around the STM trip with TLT is very exciting and has great potential. The work of L. Dee Fink and Vella would offer special value in this area.[1] I will begin with overarching themes and suggestions for STM, and then address suggestions specific to the pre-trip, trip, and post-trip phases.

STM COURSE DESIGN

The proposed process of STM course design is built around the idea of helping STM trip leaders to design significant learning experiences. As we learned from our study of TLT, the experience of a disorienting dilemma such as an STM trip sets the stage for significant personal transformation. That transformation is not automatic. If the STM trip is not a part of a larger process that involves critical reflection of the challenges faced and the exploration of new ways of acting, the opportunity for growth is largely lost. The idea of comparing classroom dynamics to the STM experience could seem a bit of a reach at times, but I believe the right vision can remedy that. Below are some helpful tips on how to design a learning experience that can all be applied to the STM process. Fink presents key questions that need to be answered when designing any learning experience:

---

1. Fink, *Creating*; Vella, *Learning to Listen*.

1. What are the important situational factors in a particular course and learning situation?

2. What should the full set of learning goals be?

3. What kinds of feedback and assessment should we provide?

4. What kinds of teaching and learning activities will suffice, in terms of achieving the full set of learning goals set?

5. Are all the components connected and integrated, that is, are they consistent with and supportive of each other?[2]

As I consider these questions, they suggest a step-by-step process for developing a curriculum that integrates with the STM process, their on-field engagement and their re-engagement with their home context. I present those developmental steps here.

Step One

The first step presented by Fink involves the STM leader thinking through the STM trip to consider the trip context, home context, skill sets needed, and individuals involved to see what kind of learning opportunities present themselves. This lines up well with Vella's first principle of assessing learning needs and resources.[3] The STM trip leader has the responsibility to identify these factors so they can each be captured as fully as possible.

Step Two

The second step involves the STM leader listing all of the learning goals for the STM experience. This means learning for pre-trip, trip, and post-trip stages and even beyond. From our reflection on TLT, we know that one general goal is positive personal transformation as a result of the disorienting dilemma of the STM trip. Once the leader has identified these goals, they can more effectively work backward toward lessons and experiences that will help achieve the desired learning goals.

---

2. Fink, *Creating*, 63.

3. Vella, *Learning to Listen*, 5–8.

Step Three

The third step gets into Vella's ideas of safety, sound relationships and even praxis a bit.[4] The STM leader needs to think through when and how assessment and feedback will take place. Our review of TLT stressed the importance of critical assessment and reflection, which Fink and Vella draw on here well. It is important to plan and account for this in advance. There have been several times I have observed significant teachable moments in the midst of a trip, but realized that I had not created the proper safety or sound relationship to allow me to address the situation appropriately. Many teachable moments will not be able to be planned, but letting the team know in advance that you plan to step in to instruct and correct when applicable can help a lot regarding expectations. When the team member knows you are working toward their greater good, correction and feedback can be received much more positively.

Step Four

Once the learning goals are set, step four is to figure out what is needed in order to accomplish those goals. This can relate to both activities and resources. The leader will want to examine what opportunities present themselves in the pre-trip, trip, and post-trip portions of the STM process.

Step Five

The fifth step is to assess how well the design fits together so far. This relates to Vella's principle of sequence and reinforcement.[5] The STM leader wants the learning to be a progressive, congruent process as opposed to a random sequence of events.

These five steps make up the initial phase of the instructional design process that focuses on building strong primary components for a course. Fink goes on to share three more steps that make up the intermediate phase of the process, which consists of assembling the components into a coherent whole:

Create a thematic structure for the course.

4. Vella, *Learning to Listen*, 8–12.
5. Vella, *Learning to Listen*, 12–14.

Select or create a teaching strategy.

Integrate the course structure and the instructional strategy to create an overall scheme of learning activities.[6]

Once the STM leader pulls all the various components of the trip together, they can then look for, or impose, a theme that ties them all together. An STM leader can choose a variety of themes from "God's Faithfulness" to "Living with Gospel Boldness." This could be especially fun when partnerships are formed that involve the same people returning to the same location year after year. Once a theme is identified, a teaching strategy can be created. The leader needs to figure out how they will go about facilitating the "course" that is the STM trip. After all of this, it is time to pull together the individual learning activities into the theme and teaching strategy.

The final phase of the process consists of finishing the important remaining tasks that include:

Develop the grading system.

Debug the possible problems.

Write the course syllabus.

Plan an evaluation of the course and of your teaching.[7]

Once the course/trip design is in place, the STM leader needs to decide what feedback will look like, which relates well to Vella's idea of praxis.[8] Then comes time to review the trip process for problems and issues that need addressing. After that, the trip needs a "syllabus" that helps communicate expectations and objectives clearly to participants. The syllabus can serve as a contract of sorts between the leader and participants. The evaluation component is important and it is best to have a planned time for internal feedback from the team as well as outside input from other staff when possible. Fink holds that it is best to work through each of these steps in order as each step forms the basis for all subsequent steps.

An added bonus comes when Fink summarizes the key changes he recommends to teachers:

- Set more ambitious goals.

---

6. Fink, *Creating*, 67.

7. Fink, *Creating*, 67.

8. Vella, *Learning to Listen*, 14–15.

- Enlarge the kinds of learning activities being used. Engage the student with both experiences and reflections that stimulate learning.

- Create rich learning experiences.

- Provide multiple opportunities for in-depth reflection on the learning process.

- Find alternative ways to introduce students to the content of the course.

- Create a coherent and meaningful course structure. Identify four to seven important concepts for the course and build the overall structure around them.

- Select or create a dynamic instructional strategy. Put learning activities into a particular sequence that can build on each other.[9]

I find summarized "best practice" feedback like this to often be of great value. The first item of change offered by Fink gets off to a great start by highlighting a major theme of this paper, that STM leaders think of STM as something far bigger than simply a trip to lead. The goal is not to simply get a group of adults overseas and back safely. The goal is nothing short of transformative, life-long change in all participants and national partners.

The second through fifth recommendations all relate to the idea of taking some risks and thinking with creativity when it comes to learning activities and processes. The sixth and seventh both help give the teacher some areas to focus on. I appreciate this as his original twelve-step plan could likely be very overwhelming to many trip leaders.

TAXONOMY OF SIGNIFICANT LEARNING

According to TLT, a good course is one that:

- Challenges students to significant kinds of learning.

- Uses active forms of learning.

- Has teachers who care—about the subject, their students, and about teaching and learning.

- Has teachers who interact well with students.

9. Fink, *Creating*, 151.

- Has a good system of feedback, assessment, and grading.[10]

This list does a good job of summarizing many of the principles discussed so far in a way that an STM leader could use without being overwhelmed. Of course, each point warrants greater explanation in order to be useful. An explanation of various forms of significant learning is still to come in this dissertation, as is some discussion of active forms of learning. That said, active forms of learning as well as teachers who care and interact and have a good system of feedback have been covered well by both Cranton and Vella so far. Next, I will discuss a taxonomy of significant learning as shared by Fink:

- Foundational Knowledge: Understanding and remembering information and ideas

- Application: Skills; Thinking critically, creatively, and practically; Managing projects

- Integration: Connecting ideas, people, and realms of life

- Human Dimension: Learning about oneself and others

- Caring: Developing new feelings, interests, and values

- Learning How to Learn: Becoming a better student; Inquiring about a subject; Self-directing learners.[11]

Foundational Knowledge

Foundational knowledge refers to students' ability to understand and remember specific information and ideas. This is the basic understanding that is needed for other kinds of learning to take place.[12] When it comes to an STM trip, this would be details regarding trip logistics as well as culture, language, and perhaps ministry as well. For example, I typically have trip participants read a few chapters from *When Helping Hurts*[13] to help shape their thinking regarding our role in the lives of South Sudanese nationals.

---

10. Fink, *Creating*, 28. Since STM is not a typical classroom learning environment, the idea of grading will likely be inappropriate. This does not negate the need for and importance of assessment, evaluation, and feedback.

11. Fink, *Creating*, 30. Fink refers to this process as an actual taxonomy for learning.

12. Fink, *Creating*, 31.

13. Corbett and Fikkert, *When Helping Hurts*.

The reading portion, without accompanying dialogue, would be foundational knowledge.

Application

Application is the idea of learning to engage in some new kind of action. This is the step of making learning useful.[14] The application phase of significant learning is often where the disorienting dilemma of TLT will take place. In our context, the STM trip is a primary place for this.

STM trips are intensely application rich, the biggest issue is what is being applied and for how long. If a skill is learned in the pre-trip stages, applied during the trip, then lost post-trip, it is worthy to question the value of that skill. Application should involve putting potential into motion; the more impact and longer lasting that motion, the better.

Integration

Integration is the idea of the learner seeing connection between different things, ideas, or realms of life. This is the step that helps make learning powerful, particularly on an intellectual level.[15] This is a stage of significant learning that fits well into the later stages of TLT following the disorienting dilemma.

Integration is something I believe could be a tremendous benefit of STM, but ends up lost in most cases. Integration happens when a participant realizes that living as a missionary does not have to be limited to an overseas context. When the participant realizes that they can also live as a missionary at home, this unlocks a new level of learning and application. The student has officially transcended the classroom.

Human Dimension

Human dimension is the dimension of learning where the learner learns something new about themselves or others in a way that enables them to function and interact more effectively. This phase of learning helps the

14. Fink, *Creating*, 31.
15. Fink, *Creating*, 31.

learner see the human significance of what they are learning.[16] On an STM this could be when a participant sees someone's life changed upon hearing the gospel. This could also be internal change that takes place for the participant upon experiencing an entirely new culture and outlook on life. These are changes not uncommon for STM trips, but the issue remains as to how lasting of a lesson they are.

Caring

Caring is the phase of learning when a learning experience changes how the learner cares for something. The change could come in the form of new feelings, interests, or values. When the learner begins to care about something, they then have the energy and motivation to learn and implement the learning even more in their lives.[17] This idea of caring fits with the idea of integration already mentioned, but takes it a bit further. Integration would be when the participant sees a connection beyond the initial application and caring would be when they take willful action in that new direction. Perhaps someone recognizes the power of the gospel in a new way and wants to live their life differently when they get back home in light of that.

Learning How to Learn

In the course of learning, the learner can begin to learn about the process of learning itself. This is when the learner begins to learn how to become a self-directed learner. This dimension of learning enables the learner to continue their education in the future and do so with even greater effectiveness.[18] Few people would walk away from an STM trip having advanced to this level as a result of the trip, unless they have quality follow-up. The trip could likely serve as a significant disorienting dilemma, but the process of dialogue and praxis are still needed in order to capture and bring about lasting life change. The idea of learning how to learn is indeed life changing.

16. Fink, *Creating*, 31–32.
17. Fink, *Creating*, 32.
18. Fink, *Creating*, 32.

When a learning experience promotes all six of these aspects of learning, it can truly be deemed a significant learning experience.[19] I strive to see this to become commonplace among STM trips.

PRINCIPLES FOR EFFECTIVE ADULT LEARNING

As seen in Chapter 2, Cranton does a great job of laying out the ideas and even some tips for conducting transformational learning. I think Vella does an excellent job of honing a process well for what practical steps can look like in the application of TLT. Adult learning is best achieved in dialogue.[20] Vella goes on to layout twelve principles to guide the educator in the process of adult learning:

1. Needs assessment: participation of the learners in naming what is to be learned.

2. Safety in the environment and the process: educators create a context for learning. That context can be made safe.

3. Sound relationships between teacher and learner and among learners.

4. Sequence of content and reinforcement.

5. Praxis: action with reflection or learning by doing.

6. Respect for learners as decision makers.

7. Ideas, feelings, and actions: cognitive, affective, and psychomotor aspects of learning.

8. Immediacy of the learning.

9. Clear roles and role development.

10. Teamwork and use of small groups.

11. Engagement of the learners in what they are learning.

12. Accountability: how do they know they know?[21]

---

19. Fink, *Creating*, 32.
20. Vella, *Learning to Listen*, 3.
21. Vella, *Learning to Listen*, 4.

Needs Assessment

Listening to learners' wants and needs can help shape any program that wants to offer immediate usefulness to adults. It is best that this dialogue begins way before the course does.[22] A helpful tool for needs assessment is the question: "Who needs what as defined by whom?"[23] This question helps get at a key issue regarding who is truly the decision maker in the course, the teacher or the learner.

A dynamic of STM that can potentially hinder the opportunity for growth on the part of the participant is that many people sign-up for STM with the desire to help someone else. Many show up with the intention of giving but as Corbett and Fikkert have asserted, that does not mean they are humble enough to receive and learn.[24] This is important to consider when applying Vella's assessment question in the previous paragraph. If the trip participant does not believe they need anything, learning will be very difficult.

An example of answering Vella's assessment question for one of my STM trips to South Sudan could be, "Brian needs to learn to prepare better for his teaching opportunities, according to Mike."[25] In order to make statements like this, the trip leader needs to know the participant on some level. The better the leader knows the learner, the more effective the learning experience has the potential to be. This raises a problem for many STM trips. Most STM trips that I have been on or led are not formed out of relationships that can afford this kind of insight. In addition, most of the pre-trip portion of any trip is fully focused on logistically preparing for the trip itself. This allows little opportunity for observation that can lead to an ability to answer Vella's assessment question in a quality way.

The reality is that both teacher and learner have responsibility in the needs assessment. The adult learner has responsibility to explain their context and needs while the teacher has the role of observing and listening to the learner as thoroughly as possible. The goal of the teacher is to find out what the learner already knows and what they think they need or want to know. By this means the teacher can best understand what they have

---

22. Vella, *Learning to Listen*, 5.

23. Vella, *Learning to Listen*, 5.

24. Corbett and Fikkert, *When Helping Hurts*.

25. This is a fictitious example.

to offer the learner.[26] Again, this kind of relationship presumes the STM participant has the intention of learning and seeing the STM process as more than simply the trip. When that is the case, the leader and the learner can collaborate to create more optimal learning experiences.

Safety

Safety means that the design of the learning tasks, the environment, and the design of groups and materials all convey to the adult learners that the learning experience being offered will work for them. Essentially, this means that the context is safe for them to be vulnerable and learn.[27] Vella goes on to give five traits that can help create a feeling of safety for the learner:

1. Trust in the competence of the design of the training and the teacher enables the learner to feel safe. The teacher can help this process by making their experience and competence clear.

2. Trust in the feasibility and relevance of course objectives help the learner feel safe. It is helpful to not only go over the objectives, but to explain and discuss them with learners.

3. Allowing learners to find their voices in small groups increases safety. Small groups are generally less intimidating and allow people the opportunity to share when they otherwise might not have in front of a larger group.

4. Trust in the sequence of activities can build safety. When the learner is able to conquer easier tasks early on, they will feel more comfortable taking on more difficult tasks later.

5. An environment that is non-judgmental will help assure safety. Intentional affirmation of the learner by the teacher is very helpful as well.[28]

In order to question existing values and assumptions the learner needs to feel safe so that they can safely let their guard down. To question existing values and assumptions is to risk judgment from self and others. For this

---

26. Vella, *Learning to Listen*, 5–6.

27. Vella, *Learning to Listen*, 8.

28. Vella, *Learning to Listen*, 9–10.

to take place well, there needs to be an environment of safety. First and foremost the trip leader has responsibility to create this environment, but trip participants also have a significant role in maintaining it.

Sound Relationships

Core traits of sound learning relationships are respect, safety, open communication, listening, and humility. The teacher-learner relationship functions best when it transcends personal differences and preferences.[29] The learner benefits greatly when they know that the teacher is on their side. The STM leader can help the process by making it very clear that their desire is to serve and work toward the betterment of the STM participant. The leader can also help advance this by being personally vulnerable as well as not judging the participant for having different views and thoughts. It is relationships like these that can help the learner during the important critical assessment that follows a disorienting dilemma.

Sequence and Reinforcement

The learning process is best when sequenced from easy to difficult and simple to complex. A good sequence is one that orders things to be taught from simple to complex issues and from group-supported to solo efforts. Good reinforcement means that facts, skills, and attitudes are repeated in diverse, engaging, and interesting ways until they are learned.[30] A standard STM trip affords this develop fairly naturally. For most, the most difficult step is living a changed life once they are back home. The pre-trip portion is a time of setting expectations and experiencing mostly low level challenges. The trip itself is typically considered the greatest challenge of the process, but I do not believe that is true in most cases. The idea of sequence and reinforcement works very well with the nature of an STM, but once again shows how important planning and preparation is on the part of the STM trip leader.

29. Vella, *Learning to Listen*, 10–11.
30. Vella, *Learning to Listen*, 12–13.

Praxis

Praxis essentially means "action with reflection." There is strong consensus among educators that doing is the best way for adults to learn anything. Praxis is doing with built-in reflection.[31] Similarly, TLT teaches the importance of self-examination following disorienting dilemma. Debrief is a common trait in most STM trips. The quality would vary greatly from trip to trip and organization to organization but it would be unusual to have a complete lack of debrief. When done well, debrief can be a great example of praxis. This is an important part of the process in all phases of the STM but I would contend it is greatest post-trip when the greatest opportunity for life change takes place.

Respect for Learners as Decision Makers

Adult learners are decision makers when it comes to their own learning and in most areas of their lives.[32] Teachers need to respect learners as someone to empower as opposed to an object to be lectured to or taught. This echoes Cranton's focus on the empowerment of the learner in TLT. This makes the role of the trip leader more challenging, but increases the potential impact of the learning experience. The goal of learning is not to reinforce the power gap between teacher and student but to elevate the student to a higher level of ability and understanding. In some cases, this may mean surpassing the teacher. The STM trip leader needs to be willing to allow for this development. Empowering a learner like this requires individual attention and can be a lot of effort.

Ideas, Feelings, Actions

Another principle of effective adult education is that the learning process should engage the mind, emotions, and muscles to give attention to the cognitive, affective, and psychomotor aspects of adult learning. By engaging all three of these areas, teachers can help overcome the common mistake of formal education that turns learning into a deluge of information and data with no reflection.[33] This is where planning an STM can get especially

31. Vella, *Learning to Listen*, 14.
32. Vella, *Learning to Listen*, 15.
33. Vella, *Learning to Listen*, 17.

interesting from a planning and learning opportunity standpoint. I am not sure of any STM that would not naturally engage the mind, emotions, and muscles. I personally have never been on a STM that does not involve a lot of activity even if that's just a lot of walking. Every STM trip involves going somewhere. Emotions seem to be among the most engaged of the three if my experiences are any indication. The mind may be the area that gets the least attention. Trip leaders would be wise to assess the trip and if necessary create situations that are sure to stimulate the minds of participants.

Immediacy

Most adults are busy and learn much more effectively when they can see the immediate usefulness of what they are learning. This does not mean that sequence and reinforcement should be subverted, but useful and actionable learning should always be in view.[34] The STM trip leader needs to make it a point to identify the relevance of what is being learned. It can be easy for participants to think of STM as a one-time thing that only has relevance "over there," but the trip leader has the responsibility to help them understand how the STM experience has great significance for their life for the long-term.

Clear Roles

It is important for adult learners to understand and feel the human equality that exists between learner and teacher. The learner needs to be free to disagree, question, and challenge the professor and other learners. This freedom and clear understanding of roles is critical in effective dialogue.[35] This also echoes of Cranton's call to the empowerment of the learner according to TLT. The trip participant needs to know what their roles are and what the expectations are of them. The learners also need to have the freedom to express conflicting thoughts and opinions. This can be tricky with STM trips, particularly in sensitive cultural situations. The leader has the role of building in safe times for things like this to make sure disagreements are addressed in an appropriate manner and time.

34. Vella, *Learning to Listen*, 19.
35. Vella, *Learning to Listen*, 20.

Teamwork

Teamwork is significant in adult education for the safety and shared responsibility that it brings. The greater the safety and the shared responsibility, the more effective the team is.[36] Teams are an integral part of virtually any STM trip, which makes the presence of teamwork very accessible, but still not a given. Safety and shared responsibility are both concepts that have already been discussed and the STM trip leader will need to work hard to facilitate them. A particular challenge is that STM trips are normally so short that building real trust and safety can be difficult. Even so, the disruptive nature of the shared STM experience tends to bond people much faster than would be the case over the same time period under normal conditions at home.[37]

Engagement

Engagement represents the act of the learner actively participating in the reality of what they are learning. This participation could be true on a decision-making or implementation level.[38] This also echoes strongly of Cranton's idea of learner empowerment in TLT. In this case the learner is not passively receiving information, but actively involved in activities and dialogues surrounding the learning focus.

On an STM this could mean engaging a trip participant in how evangelism should be done as opposed to force-feeding an existing model. As with other learning components, this can be especially challenging due to the short timeframe of STM trips and training. This is another opportunity for me to call on STM trip leaders to not make the trip the sole focus of the STM experience. To get the full value out of the STM experience, I propose that there needs to be a greater focus on the development of the trip participant.

Accountability

One of the foremost principles of adult learning is accountability. Both the teacher is accountable to the learner, the learner to the teacher, and the

36. Vella, *Learning to Listen*, 22.

37. Hirsch, *Forgotten Ways*, 220–21.

38. Vella, *Learning to Listen*, 24–25.

learners to their colleagues. Accountability is the learning principle that brings the other eleven together.[39] Learning is not one-sided and it is not exclusive to the learner, just as teaching is not one-sided and exclusive to the teacher. The teacher is facilitating a journey of mutual growth and benefit for all involved.

For STM, the principle of accountability builds off of the last principle of teamwork. As people on the team carry different responsibilities within the framework of a shared mission and experience there are great opportunities to observe and instruct each other. The team, or community, can serve to encourage one another, correct one another, and even mutually instruct one another. When there is a strong team, there is room for great accountability, which paves the way for transformative learning.

Summary

This new look at the STM leader as teacher-shepherd can appear daunting, but this is not necessary. Much of the hard work of designing transformative learning experiences for a trip can be repeated over and over once initially created. I would encourage churches and mission agencies to standardize some of the processes mentioned here and create a resource tool chest from which trip leader can draw ideas and techniques. I think of this extra upfront work as similar to buying a higher priced, higher quality item of clothing. It may cost more initially, but it lasts a lot longer. The lower quality item is less expensive but you will need to replace it earlier and more often. In the end, it can pay big long-term dividends to pay the early price of laying strong foundations for STM trips that utilize TLT and adult learning methods.

I will now turn my focus from overarching STM themes and suggested changes to specifics for each phase of STM. I will discuss best practices and suggestions for the pre-trip, trip, and post-trip portions of STM. The pre-trip and post-trip sections will be notably more involved than the trip portion since there are less gaps to be filled in current trip practice. In addition, many of the recommendations based upon TLT come to bear more heavily in the pre-trip and post-trip stages of STM.

---

39. Vella, *Learning to Listen*, 25.

Chapter 6

STM Best Practices

I WOULD LIKE TO present a new method of viewing and approaching STM that places a full focus on the long-term for all involved. This proposed model aims to enhance the long-term impact of STM internationally and domestically. According to my research, there is little shortage of literature addressing ways to increase the value and impact of STM internationally. As a result, while I will address the trip portion of STM briefly, my main focus will be on the long-term aspect for the trip participant. Some of the subjects below have been addressed on some level in the practical section on TLT. In these cases, this information will be summarized.

PRE-TRIP

This section will address best practices and suggestions for the pre-trip portion of STM based upon my findings. I discuss the importance of expectations and participant selection. Creating an STM experience with long-term impact should begin from the very start of the process.

Expectations

It is beneficial for expectations of the trip on the part of the leader and participants to be made very clear, even before people apply for the trip. The STM process is not merely about a trip overseas, but a process of discipleship and transformation. In order for participants to properly engage in the process from a discipleship perspective, particularly after the trip is over, they need to have alignment with the bigger picture goal of the STM process.

In a similar way, the trip leader functions best when they have the proper expectations. Leading STM well is not simply about handling logistics and being a good chaperon. I believe that the STM leader who wants to maximize the experience would do well to view themselves as a teacher-shepherd on mission. The leader has the task of both designing integrated transformative learning experiences as they simultaneously shepherd participants through the greater process. This new approach requires more work, but the potential reward is very high. This new method has the potential to create a STM trip experience that offers much greater value to the nationals they serve because the participants are much better equipped. In addition, participants are engaged in a process to help facilitate and better ensure life-long growth as a disciple of Jesus and a missionary. Lastly, the pool of potential missionaries at home and abroad on both a short-term and long-term basis gets greatly multiplied.

Participant Selection

From the beginning, it is important for the STM leader to view the STM trip process as a learning experience to design, not just a trip to conduct. This will impact the people allowed to come on the trip and how their time is spent before, during, and after the trip. The STM leader has the task of working to create strong relationships and social capital with and among the STM team. The better the leader gets to know the participants, the better the leader can design the STM discipleship process. Getting to know trip participants involves three primary steps:

1. Informal interview of participant

2. Discussions with referrals

3. Observation of participant in ministry and team contexts

The informal interview could be part of the selection process, but preferably not limited to that. A good practice is for the trip leader to periodically connect with each team member on an individual level for the purpose of relationship-building, feedback, and assessment. The time with referrals is somewhat similar but more front-end loaded. The trip leader could benefit greatly by learning from participant referrals. Valuable information could be gained about not only whether the person is a good fit for the trip, but also where their greatest opportunities to serve and grow are. Finally, the trip leader observes the trip participant as they interact with the team and in ministry service opportunities as possible. These observations can contribute a lot to how best to lead the participant in a way that leads to the greatest amount of growth and transformation.

Summary

I want to highlight some best practices found in my literature review and field research that relates to pre-trip training. In Chapter 1, I pieced together some best practices from the literature that a good pre-trip training can consider, including the following preparations:

- Adequate long-term vision
- Selfless focus regarding impact
- Proper motivation for going
- Healthy gospel focus
- Proper expectations with eternity in mind
- Dependence on God, healthy theology
- Assigning journaling tasks to promote reflection
- Holding periodic group discussions to promote dialogue
- Spending as much time studying the context you are going to as you do preparing for ministry activities
- Providing readings and instruction on other related topics, such as poverty
- Having people who have gone on the trip previously visit with the team before the trip
- Inviting people from the context you are going to come and spend time with your group

There are few things I would add to this list:

- Preparation and training for ministry to be done on the trip (see Table 2 and 3 in Chapter 4)

- An expectation to continue working after the trip to build on the work God has done in their life (see Table 1 in Chapter 2)
- Strong foundation in fasting and prayer (see Table 2 in Chapter 4)

This represents a good starting point for what lessons to consider when designing a pre-trip training. Through my research found in Chapter 4, I discovered that these were the things that participants found most helpful:

1. Culture and history background
2. Creation to Christ evangelism training
3. Prayer
4. Trip logistics and planning

Culture and history background outranked the second result by greater than two to one. There are three primary things that the subjects especially appreciated and wanted: preparation for culture, ministry, and logistics. I am encouraged to see that prayer was mentioned four times. Note that all the training focus is on the trip itself and little thought is given to the personal transformation of the participants. These same participants found the following to be the greatest needs that were still lacking after pre-trip training ended:

1. Practicing Creation to Christ story for evangelism
2. More training in how to connect cross-culturally

These two needs correlate directly with what participants found most helpful. It appears there is a high priority on the ability to connect and relate to nationals and to do ministry effectively. The participants interviewed seem to believe they need, or would like, more of both. I believe that underneath this desire for more training is also a fear of the unknown. Most trip participants in my research were travelling to a war-torn, undeveloped nation of South Sudan for the first time. This, like most STM trips, tends to be a very disorienting experience as described in TLT. It seems that participants are anticipating this dilemma and attempting to circumvent it as much as possible. STM leaders would be wise to discuss this concern with trip participants and work to strike the balance between proper preparation and the benefits of healthy disorientation.

TRIP

The actual trip portion of STM is unsurprisingly the piece that receives the majority of the focus in the literature and accordingly will not receive as much focus in my conclusion here. My research has spoken heavily into what best practices of a trip can look like. The data shows that the top four factors for building stronger, mutually beneficial relationships are:

1. Serving together

2. Down time together

3. Equality in partnership

4. Serving the same God

A key theme here is the equality and partnership between STM participants and the nationals they serve with on STM. The idea of equality is highlighted in the idea of mutual brokenness by Corbett and Fikkert.[1] My research also shows that the greatest catalysts for growth for STM participants are:

1. Time with South Sudanese national director (Pastor A)

2. Passion of faith of South Sudanese

3. On-going relationships with South Sudanese

4. Boldness of South Sudanese with the Gospel

5. Conversations with South Sudanese

All of these come through strong relationships with nationals. The lasting results that participants claimed to walk away with were:

1. Perspective

2. Challenged

3. Encouragement

4. Stronger in evangelism

5. Vision for future

It is easy to notice all of these are very subjective and consist of little to no concrete change. The only potential exception is the idea of growing stronger in evangelism, but there is no evidence in my research to show

1. Corbett and Fikkert, *When Helping Hurts*, 64.

there was actually any real growth here. According to Ver Beek's research, it is not unreasonable to assume there was little real change here.[2] This positive sentiment is a wonderful thing, but highlights the need for some form of post-trip follow-up to help turn it into something constructive and lasting.

There is another point I would like to address. For STM to be mutually beneficial and consist of truly inter-dependent partnerships, North American believers will need humility and a willingness to learn. There is no more room for ethnocentrism and paternalism on the part of the North American Church as the Church in much of the developing world has grown into adulthood. Even so, God has blessed the North American Church with much and therefore much should be expected. STM participants should partner with fellow believers in the developing world as equals without a sense of superiority.[3] This hits at the heart of a STM focus that is mutually beneficial for all involved. The reality is that both the trip participants and the national partners have great things to offer and also have notable needs. It is a wonderful thing when the two are able to serve side-by-side and see those gifts and needs find alignment through mutually beneficial relationships.

POST-TRIP

This section will address best practices and suggestions for the post-trip portion of STM based upon my findings. I will also share the vision for Missionary Academy (MA), a proposed option to meet the need for post-trip training for STM. After sharing the vision, I touch on the model and application of Mission Academy (MA) thus far as a means of capturing and building upon the unique opportunity that the disorienting dilemma of STM offers.

Based upon the literature review in Chapter 1, some best practices for post-trip follow-up training are:

- Clear follow-up structure and process
- Ongoing accountability
- Ongoing encouragement

2. Ver Beek, "Sapling," 479–80.
3. Cuellar, "Bigger Than You Think," 285–56.

- Intentional reflection and evaluation of trip experience
- Community dialogue with focus on action and life-change

The most significant takeaway from the literature on post-trip training was the fact that there was so little material dedicated to the subject. My field research reinforces this gap. Over 73 percent of people surveyed said they received no follow-up training at all and those who did receive follow-up described times of trip debrief as opposed to actual on-going training. Not one person surveyed mentioned having any on-going training after their trip was over.

According to TLT, this means that there is an incredible opportunity that is being missed by STM practitioners. In TLT, disorienting dilemma is the first step in the transformation process but popular STM literature and practice seem comfortable leaving it as an unfinished last step. In order for STM to truly bring about lasting, positive life change in trip participants, TLT says there must be substantive post-trip follow-up and training. In the next section, I will share my thoughts on one possible solution.

MISSIONARY ACADEMY PROPOSED

There are many specific, tangible takeaways from this research based upon my findings. In regard to post-trip training, it is clear that there is a significant deficiency in this regard. Subjects show a strong need and desire for on-going training that can help them to capitalize on the catalysts from the trip. It has been suggested that some kind of structure that provides encouragement and accountability is what is most needed. It is out of this scenario that MA was initially birthed. MA is intended to not only follow-up a STM trip but in many cases to also serve as a precursor. In this way, the relationship between STM and MA is actually a circular one as opposed to linear. MA should follow every STM trip, but it can also serve as a means of cultivating and training future STM leaders and participants.

My proposal to help fill the gap that exists in STM regarding post-trip training is a project I have come to refer to as MA. In 2012, I began hosting STM trip meetings after the trip was over. We would gather and talk about what it could look like to have a greater missionary presence in our home contexts. These meetings were enjoyable and pretty well attended initially. Over time, attendance began to fade and I quickly saw the need for greater structure. In my experience, people tend to do better in commitment when there is a clear set of expectations. In 2014, I officially launched the first MA cohort with six others and myself.

MA is a six-month long program that meets monthly. The reason for only one meeting per month is the problem of overloading already busy schedules and burning people out. MA has three primary goals:

1. Increase gospel fluency
2. Cultivate gospel-centered community
3. Promote gospel activity

Vision

The vision of MA is that anytime someone goes on an STM trip, they are beginning a lifelong process of discipleship as opposed to simply going on a short trip. People come on trips out of their desire to serve the Lord and bring the hope of the gospel to people who may otherwise not know it. The goal of MA is to build upon that initial spark that led them to go on the trip and see it kindled during the trip and then grow into a strong, enduring fire upon returning home. This fire will not happen by accident. Once back home, these trip participants will have the opportunity to join a like-minded, intentional group of people as a part of MA. This group will gather for the purpose of cultivating a more Christ-centered life.

At MA they will learn and grow in Gospel Fluency, the ability to fluidly speak the good news of Christ into any situation. Gospel fluency is measured by a person's ability to, in any situation answer the question, "How is Christ good news for this person in this situation?" They will begin to foster a Gospel Community around them of other like-minded believers who will continue to provide them the encouragement and accountability they need long after MA has ended. Their Gospel Diet will be evaluated to get a better understanding of what messages they are consuming every day and how those messages affect their ability to live in a Christ-centered way. They will learn to speak Gospel Fluent phrases to themselves to help build their Gospel Identity more firmly in truth. In all of this they will become more Gospel Active by regularly and routinely spreading the Gospel into their everyday activities and conversations.

Beyond these things they will learn to better interact with people cross-culturally, particularly beyond the church/Christian sub-culture that can be so far removed from the everyday people they interact with. The intention of MA is to train participants in a way that is easily reproducible. In South Sudan, we currently implement the three-thirds model where every training opportunity is divided into three parts consisting of review, new material, and practice. This model has been proven very effective in facilitating reproducible training.[4] A similar model is built into the format of MA. Ultimately, my desire is to see models similar to MA adopted by churches and other mission organizations to help mobilize the approximately 1.6 million adults every year on STM as missionaries in their home communities once they return back home. If just ten percent of these people can be mobilized back home, that will translate to 160,000 new missionaries entering the mission field every year here at home.

As discussed above, MA has the potential to provide the structure and environment needed to help participants capture and build on what God did in their lives during their STM. For six months they will have a focused place to process and work through what it means to be a missionary at home. Even more, they will have the encouragement and accountability they need to stay the course.

Most of the time the STM trip is seen as an end in itself. All the buildup and prep is focused on the trip itself and what will happen while away. In this format, everything revolves around the trip and process of discipleship ends once everyone returns home. I desire to shift the dynamic to where the STM is seen as important step in a much bigger process of discipleship through MA. Conversely, discipleship at home in the U.S. seems to often lack the "going" part of the Great Commandment. MA has the opportunity to offer a more balanced and informed kind of discipleship that helps participants gain a deeper understanding of the gospel and salvation as a whole.[5]

I believe the implications on missiology are enormous. In 2005, approximately 1.6 million U.S. adults traveled abroad on STM.[6] Imagine if the opportunity of the disorienting dilemma could be captured upon STM participants returning home to the U.S. That would mean a flood of new missionaries living actively on mission in their workplaces and communities every year. I believe this can happen if STM trips have a leader with enough vision to not let the work the Lord did in their lives during the

4. Smith and Kai, *T4T*, 125.

5. Lunde, *Following Jesus*, 280–81.

6. Priest, Robert, *Effective*, ii.

STM trip die due to lack of support when they return home. I believe this research has the potential to have an impact like this, and even more.

Model

The purpose of MA is to help people to better understand, live, and proclaim the gospel of Jesus Christ. A typical MA will last for six months with one meeting each month. I often explain this number of meetings and the time frame are not magical, but are minimums. The goal is to meet often enough, over enough time to help develop and establish new skills and even community. A group could meet weekly or bi-weekly and could go on for longer than six months. I still believe the best model will be for pre-existing communities, like small groups, to go through the MA process together.

Most meetings last for around two hours and consist of some relaxed catch-up time followed by a time of debrief over how things have gone since the last meeting. This time will include a lot of personal coaching as well as encouragement. Afterwards, there is a time for teaching new material.

Application

The primary goals of MA are to provide encouragement and accountability around the idea of training participants to be active missionaries at home.[7] MA is built around three primary lessons and activities of growing in gospel fluency, cultivating gospel community, and chasing your "far five."

Gospel fluency and cultivating gospel-centered community are both top priorities of MA. A person's far five are five people in someone's life that are far from God. These are five people that students are actively praying for and pursuing with the love of God. MA consists of the lessons, activities, and community that supports and fosters these three core principles. In the following sections, I will share some results and experiences based upon the first two MA six-month sessions, which we refer to as "cohorts." In these sessions, we work together through both the disorienting dilemmas of the STM trip and the often recurring disorienting dilemmas that occur as people begin to live and speak boldly in the faith.

---

7. Ver Beek, "Sapling," 492–95.

Cohort One

Every member of the first MA cohort had overseas mission experience and six of them had actually gone on an STM trip with me to South Sudan. Of the seven total people that participated in the first cohort, four actually completed the program. The three who did not finish had too many scheduling conflicts. We have one meeting each month for six months, each meeting lasted around two hours. The meetings were always very casual and took place in our very small organization offices. We really had a lot of fun.

At each meeting I would introduce a new lesson and a new practical skill or exercise we could do on our own to help us to grow as missionaries. This teaching time was secondary to time spent providing encouragement and accountability to the cohort. No curriculum can prepare a student for every scenario they face in the world. These times of debrief allowed students to share successes and failures in a safe environment and receive personalized and specific encouragement and direction to help them grow.

Some feedback I received from students was that they enjoyed the ideas taught and the exercises given, but they struggled with discipline and follow through on their end. One suggestion was to actually give worksheets out in class to be completed as homework. This would make the assignments more tangible and remove extra steps on the part of students. Students also expressed difficulty in expanding their ability to recognize and capitalize on opportunities to share the gospel. They said they needed more practice and help with creativity in this regard. The idea of having five key people in our lives to pray for and reach out to was considered a great strength of the program, but greater accountability was needed there. Lastly, students also expressed the need for more encouragement and ideas for cultivating a community of like-minded gospel-focused people around them. In addition to this, I observed a notable loss of momentum the longer we went between meetings and as we neared the end of the overall program. I interpret this to mean there is not enough engagement between meetings to keep students stimulated and that the later part of the program was not as engaging as the earlier meetings.

Cohort Two

In cohort two, there were four students and none had travelled overseas with my organization or me in the past. There was also no expressed interest in traveling overseas on mission in the future. All four students had the desire to be more active in sharing the gospel in their home contexts. This was an exciting expansion in the MA vision. While the focus is on returning STM participants, the program can serve people regardless of mission background or affiliation. The disorienting dilemmas associated with living and speaking boldly on behalf of the gospel offers many opportunities for personal growth and transformation.

One notable shift from cohort one to two has been the provision of a written curriculum and handouts. The benefits of this have been very evident as students have been visibly more engaged in the process over time and I have seen much less momentum loss. I also shifted the focus of meetings from teaching new material to a heavier concentration on coaching and encouraging students. I have found that more time debriefing and working through experiences helps improve both engagement and application.

SUMMARY

My review of the literature and personal research has positively affirmed that there is not only a gap in STM literature regarding post-trip follow-up, but also in practice. The vision of MA in building upon the disorienting dilemma of STM is one that I find very exciting with very significant potential. In our first two cohorts of MA, we have been very encouraged by the impact on participants. Equally encouraging, I have personally seen great growth in my understanding of and confidence in sharing the gospel. As we have spoken with other churches and ministries, the interest in and need for a resource like MA has been almost universally affirmed.

An especially exciting element has been the application and interest in MA by people not even associated with STM. This offers an additional application for MA. Not only can MA be a great follow-up for a trip, but it can be a great program for cultivating future STM trip leaders and participants. It is my hope that this dissertation will serve as a great resource in helping others launch similar programs. Eventually, maybe we will have the joy of seeing ten percent or greater of STM with a program like MA and hundreds of thousands of people will be launched across the U.S. as missionaries for Jesus Christ in their homes, offices, and communities.

Conclusion

THE MISSIOLOGICAL IMPLICATIONS AND potential impact of a new model for STM that includes post-trip training along the lines of MA are significant and have already been mentioned. Even so, the numbers bear repeating. If just ten percent of all U.S. STM participants participated in this form of STM process that would equate to approximately 160,000 new missionaries "entering" the U.S. every year. That kind of growth could easily be expected to produce fruit that few can imagine. To see results such as these, change in practice must take place.

RECOMMENDATIONS FOR STM

I have proposed some changes with regard to STM, mostly in relation to the pre- and post-trip stages. In the pre-trip stage, I spoke of the importance of proper expectations on the part of the leader and trip participant from the very beginning. Each should have the view that STM is a discipleship process that is bigger than a trip that can have significant, lasting impact. This factors back into selection as well. Participation in STM should not be an open invitation, but a careful selection of people ready to contribute and eager to learn and grow as a missionary.

To aide in this process, I have turned to TLT and adult learning theory. TLT offers STM trip leaders a helpful guide for theory and practice in how to lead trip participants in life transformation. A core aspect of TLT is the idea of the disorienting dilemma as central in life transformation. STM has the potential to be that disorienting dilemma for anyone who participates.

With regard to the post-trip stage of STM, I proposed the idea of MA as a means of capturing the disorienting dilemma of STM using TLT and adult learning theory. Through the literature and my research, it became very evident that there is a large gap in STM when it comes to post-trip training or follow-up of any substance. In order to capture the momentum of the disorienting dilemma of the STM trip, MA was created. MA provides not only helpful training for being a missionary in home contexts, but also offers needed encouragement and accountability along the way. I dream of what the Church in the U.S. would look like if something like MA became widely adopted.

In order to change the STM culture, there is the need to push for structural and institutional change of narrative. Changing language, thinking, and practice alone is not enough.[1] Changing the STM culture is not simply an issue of better training and follow-up, but of changing the existing structure of STM and its purpose in the eyes of the institutions that promote them.[2] With this in mind, STM best practice would not have the trip as its key focus. I propose that STM should be a process of deep discipleship with a trip component geared toward establishing mutually beneficial relationships with nationals that continue year-after-year. Attempting to change the existing culture and practice of STM has been attempted and failed plenty of times.[3] One particular critique of current STM culture is emphasis on the need to do something.[4] STM participants cannot be governed by a drive to accomplish something to the point of doing damage instead of good. The narrative needs to change from Americans going to help people overseas to broken people coming together for mutual, long-lasting benefit.

RECOMMENDATIONS FOR FURTHER STUDY

For further study, I recommend a deeper look into how a focus on long-term participant growth impacts the fruitfulness of the actual STM trip. My assumption is that the trip would be a richer experience for all, but my research did not address this. I would like to see the impact of a program like MA studied. It would be nice to compare STM participants before and after MA as well as against a control group. The ability to train leaders to lead STM trips like these is of special interest to me as well. A study that tried to implement a transformative learning approach to STM would add

1. Howell, *Ethnography*, 198.
2. Howell, *Ethnography*, 204.
3. Howell, *Ethnography*, 207.
4. Howell, *Ethnography*, 208.

much to the discussion. Research into participant retention in post-trip training would be helpful. I suspect many participants would be tempted to drop off involvement once the trip was completed. A longer-term study that looked at how the new approach to STM proposed in this paper impacts the number of LTM workers sent out from a faith community would be very interesting. In addition to these thoughts, there is a tremendous amount of research that could be done on how to most effectively operate MA. All forms of methods, curriculum, and applications could be examined to help create a program that best equips STM participants for long-term missional growth and application in the U.S. I would also like to see a more comprehensive study on how STM are used globally by both churches and para-church organizations.

FINAL COMMENTS

I began this study with the purpose of exploring how to maximize STM in a way that creates the most mutually beneficial, long-term missional impact possible. As I reflect back on this dissertation, I believe significant progress has been made. I have found and shown that STM can be conducted in a way that is mutually beneficial to both trip participant and national host. I have also shown that one of the greatest gaps in the STM process is in the post-trip stage and have proposed tested solutions that have already born fruit.

The stated goal of this study was to discover best practices for structuring short-term mission experiences in a way that creates mutually beneficial, long-term missional growth in the life of participants. I believe that MA is the fulfillment of this goal. The early fruit and ongoing enthusiasm related to MA bears testimony to this.

The central research issue was to explore the life-transformative impact of STM experiences with a special focus on the long-term missional development of trip participants. This exploration led me to dive deep into the literature of STM and TLT where I found notable synergies between the two. The literature for STM and my personal research led to the conclusion that for STM to have a long-term missional impact, trip participants must have training and support that goes beyond the trip itself. I can confidently say that issue researched is much better understood now and clear, constructive steps forward have been identified.

I truly believe that STM can be a great blessing to national hosts, LTM workers, local churches back home, and the STM participants themselves. This kind of synergy will not happen accidentally or without a lot of hard work. If the narrative of STM can change from trip focused to discipleship focused we will have taken a major step forward. It is my hope that this dissertation and the ongoing legacy of MA will be used by God to help write the story of this new narrative.

Appendix A

American Interview Questions

1. Have you worked overseas before? In what capacity?

2. Were the relationships you formed with Southern Sudanese beneficial to you? How?

3. What preparation was helpful or unhelpful to you as you formed these relationships? Was there training you did not receive but would have liked to receive?

4. Do you believe the relationships you formed were beneficial to the Southern Sudanese? How?

5. What things were most helpful in forming beneficial relationships with Southern Sudanese? Least helpful?

6. How (do you hope your life will be/is your life) different now as a result of this trip and these relationships?

7. Do you expect these changes to continue into the future for you? For the Southern Sudanese?

8. What will you do to help these changes continue?

9. What follow-up training did you receive? How did it impact your ability to transfer the lessons learned on the trip into your life at home?

10. How will your involvement in church planting and community transformation specifically be different as you move forward? How did your training, before and after, influence this?

11. What things were most impactful to you in your relationship with the Southern Sudanese?

12. What things were most impactful to you about the trip as a whole?

13. What was helpful in your preparation for the trip? What was unhelpful?

14. Was something missing in your training?

15. What was helpful in your follow-up for the trip? What was unhelpful?

16. Was something missing in your follow-up training?

Appendix B

South Sudanese Interview Questions

1. Have you worked with American teams before?

2. For how long have you been working with American teams?

3. Were the relationships you formed helpful to you? How?

4. Do you believe the relationships were helpful to the Americans? How?

5. How is your life different now as a result of your time with Americans?

6. Is it easy or hard to build relationships with Americans?

7. What are things that Americans do that make building relationships with them easy or hard?

8. Tell me about a good relationship you have had with an American and how it developed.

9. Tell me about a bad relationship you have had with an American and how it developed (or did not develop).

10. When you are with the Americans, do you feel like you are working with them or for them?

11. What is your favorite thing about working with Americans?

12. What is your least favorite thing about working with Americans?

13. What is something you have wished for in your relationships with Americans that rarely or never happens?

14. How can Americans most bless you as a friend?

15. How have the relationships formed with the Americans impacted you as a church planter?

16. Do you consider yourself better equipped as a church planter as a result of the relationships you formed with the Americans? Why or why not?

Appendix C

Open-Ended and Closed-Ended Survey Questions

1. How many short-term trips have you taken to South Sudan?

2. What year was the first?

3. What year was the most recent?

4. Have you worked internationally in other capacities? (example, other mission trips/work trips to other parts of the world?)

5. If so, can you briefly give the details? (where, how often, how long)

6. Were the relationships you formed with Southern Sudanese beneficial to you?

7. How?

8. Did you receive preparation for the trip that helped you form better relationships with Southern Sudanese?

9. If so, what things were helpful?

10. Was there training that you would have liked to have received but did not?

11. If so, what do you feel like was missing?

12. Do you believe the relationships you formed were beneficial to the Southern Sudanese?

13. If so, how?

14. Do you believe the relationships you formed with Southern Sudanese were mutually beneficial?

15. If so, what do you believe was most helpful in accomplishing this? (training, preparation, circumstances, etc.)

16. Were there things that interfered with the building of mutually beneficial relationships?

17. If so, what were these things?

18. Is your life different now because of the relationships you formed?

19. If so, in what ways?

20. Do you expect these life changes to continue for you and for the Southern Sudanese?

21. Why or why not?

22. How will you help to sustain these changes?

23. Have you received any follow-up training after the trip?

24. If so, what has it consisted of and how has it been helpful?

25. Has your involvement in church planting or community development here at home changed at all as a result of this trip?

26. If so, how did your trip training influence this?

27. What things were most impactful to you in your relationship with the Southern Sudanese?

28. What things were most impactful to you about the trip as a whole?

29. What was helpful in your preparation for the trip? What was unhelpful?

30. Was something missing in your training?

31. What was helpful in your follow-up for the trip? What was unhelpful?

32. Was something missing in your follow-up training?

Bibliography

Adeney, Miriam. "The Myth of the Blank Slate: A Checklist for Short-Term Missions." In *Effective Engagement in Short-Term Missions: Doing It Right!*, edited by Robert J. Priest, 120–50. Pasadena: William Carey Library, 2008.

Barnes, Seth. "The Changing Face of the Missionary Force." In *Engaging the Church: Analyzing the Canvas of Short-Term Missions*, edited by Laurie A. Fortunak and A. Scott Moreau, 103–9. Wheaton, IL: EMIS, 2008.

Barrett, Stanley R. *Anthropology: A Student's Guide to Theory and Method.* Toronto: University of Toronto Press, 1996.

Bernard, H. Russell. *Research Methods in Anthropology: Qualitative and Quantitative Approaches.* Lanham: AltaMira, 2006.

Bessenecker, Scott. "Paul's Short-Term Church Planting: Can It Happen Again?" In *Engaging the Church: Analyzing the Canvas of Short-Term Missions*, edited by Laurie A. Fortunak and A. Scott Moreau, 32–39. Wheaton, IL: EMIS, 2008.

Blomberg, Fran. "From 'Whatever' to Wherever: Enhancing Faith Formation in Young Adults through Short-Term Missions." In *Effective Engagement in Short-Term Missions: Doing It Right!*, edited by Robert J. Priest, 590–611. Pasadena: William Carey Library, 2008.

Borthwick, Paul. "Short-Term Youth Teams: Are They Worth It?" In *Engaging the Church: Analyzing the Canvas of Short-Term Missions*, edited by Laurie A. Fortunak and A. Scott Moreau, 125–29. Wheaton, IL: EMIS, 2008.

Brookfield, Stephen. *Developing Critical Thinkers.* Edited by Alan B. Knox. The Jossey-Bass Higher Education Series and the Jossey-Bass Management Series. San Francisco: Jossey-Bass, 1987.

Brown, C. M. "Friendship Is Forever: Congregation-to-Congregation Relationships." In *Effective Engagement in Short-Term Missions: Doing It Right!*, edited by Robert J. Priest, 208–37. Pasadena: William Carey Library, 2008.

Campbell, William E., and Karl A. Smith. *New Paradigms for College Teaching.* Edina: Interaction, 1997.

Charmaz, Kathy. "Grounded Theory." In *Contemporary Field Research: Perspectives and Formulations*, edited by Robert M. Emerson, 335–52. Prospect Heights: Waveland, 2001.

Corbett, Steve, and Brian Fikkert. *When Helping Hurts: How to Alleviate Poverty without Hurting the Poor—and Yourself.* Chicago: Moody, 2009.

Bibliography

Cranton, Patricia. *Understanding and Promoting Transformative Learning: A Guide for Educators of Adults*. The Jossey-Bass Higher and Adult Education Series. San Francisco: Jossey-Bass, 2006.

Cuellar, Rolando W. "Short-Term Missions Are Bigger Than You Think: Missiological Implications for the Glocal Church." In *Effective Engagement in Short-Term Missions: Doing It Right!*, edited by Robert J. Priest, 276–89. Pasadena: William Carey Library, 2008.

Elmer, Duane. *Cross-Cultural Servanthood: Serving the World in Christlike Humility*. Downers Grove, IL: InterVarsity, 2006.

Fink, L. Dee. *Creating Significant Learning Experiences: An Integrated Approach to Designing College Courses*. Jossey-Bass Higher and Adult Education Series. San Francisco: Jossey-Bass, 2003.

Friesen, Randy. "The Long-Term Impact of Short-Term Missions." In *Engaging the Church: Analyzing the Canvas of Short-Term Missions*, edited by Laurie A. Fortunak and A. Scott Moreau, 177–84. Wheaton, IL: EMIS, 2008.

Gibbs, Graham. *Analyzing Qualitative Data*. Los Angeles: SAGE, 2007.

Heerwagen, Brian J., and Dianne Grudda. *The Next Mile: Short-Term Missions for the Long Haul*: Authentic, 2005.

Hirsch, Alan. *The Forgotten Ways: Reactivating the Missional Church*. Grand Rapids: Brazos, 2006.

Hitt, Russell T. *Jungle Pilot: The Gripping Story of Nate Saint, Martyred Missionary to Ecuador*. Grand Rapids: Discovery House, 1997.

Holstein, James A., and Jaber F. Gubrium. *The Active Interview*. Thousand Oaks: SAGE, 1995.

Howell, Brian M. *Short-Term Mission: An Ethnography of Christian Travel Narrative and Experience*. Downers Grove, IL: IVP Academic, 2012.

Johnson, Douglas H. *The Root Causes of Sudan's Civil Wars*. Bloomington: Indiana University Press, 2006.

Jorgensen, Danny L. *Participant Observation: A Methodology for Human Studies*. Newbury Park: Sage, 1989.

King, Patricia M., and Karen Strohm Kitchener. *Developing Reflective Judgment*. Edited by Ursula Delworth, *The Jossey-Bass Higher and Adult Education Series and the Jossey-Bass Social and Behavioral Science Series*. San Francisco: Jossey-Bass, 1994.

Livermore, David A. *Serving with Eyes Wide Open: Doing Short-Term Missions with Cultural Intelligence*. Grand Rapids: Baker, 2006.

Lunde, Jonathan. *Following Jesus, the Servant King: A Biblical Theology of Covenantal Discipleship*. Grand Rapids: Zondervan, 2010.

Marston, Sean. *Seeking That Missing Person*. In *Engaging the Church: Analyzing the Canvas of Short-Term Missions*, edited by Laurie A. Fortunak and A. Scott Moreau, 185–90. Wheaton, IL: EMIS, 2008.

May, Stan. "Short-Term Mission Trips Are Great, If . . . " In *Engaging the Church: Analyzing the Canvas of Short-Term Missions*, edited by Laurie A. Fortunak and A. Scott Moreau, 93–96. Wheaton, IL: EMIS, 2008.

Mezirow, Jack. *Learning as Transformation: Critical Perspectives on a Theory in Progress, The Jossey-Bass Higher and Adult Education Series*. San Francisco: Jossey-Bass, 2000.

———. "Transformative Learning as Discourse." *Journal of Transformative Education* 1 (2003) 58–63.

Bibliography

Moreau, A. Scott. "Short-Term Missions in the Context of Missions, Inc." In *Effective Engagement in Short-Term Missions: Doing It Right!*, edited by Robert J. Priest, 1–33. Pasadena: William Carey Library, 2008.

Myers, Bryant L. *Walking with the Poor: Principles and Practices of Transformational Development*. Rev. and exp. ed. Maryknoll, NY: Orbis, 2011.

Occhipinti, Laurie A. *Making a Difference in a Globalized World: Short-Term Missions That Work*. London: Rowman & Littlefield, 2014.

Park, Kyeong Sook. "Researching Short-Term Missions and Paternalism." In *Effective Engagement in Short-Term Missions: Doing It Right!*, edited by Robert J. Priest, 504–28. Pasadena: William Carey Library, 2008.

Peterson, Roger, et al. *Maximum Impact Short-Term Mission: The God-Commanded, Repetitive Deployment of Swift, Temporary, Non-Professional Missionaries*, 2003.

Priest, Kersten Bayt. "Women as Resource Brokers: Stm Trips, Social and Orgnanizational Ties, and Mutual Resource Benefits." In *Effective Engagement in Short-Term Missions: Doing It Right!*, edited by Robert J. Priest, 256–75. Pasadena: William Carey Library, 2008.

Priest, Robert J. *Effective Engagement in Short-Term Missions: Doing It Right*. Pasadena: William Carey Library, 2008.

Reese, Robert. "Short-Term Missions as Spiritual Exercise." In *Engaging the Church: Analyzing the Canvas of Short-Term Missions*, edited by Laurie A. Fortunak and A. Scott Moreau, 40–46. Wheaton, IL: EMIS, 2008.

Richardson, Rick. "The Impact of Urban Short-Term Projects on the Social Connections of Evangelical College Students." In *Effective Engagement in Short-Term Missions: Doing It Right!*, edited by Robert J. Priest, 530–56. Pasadena: William Carey Library, 2008.

Rickett, Daniel. "Short-Term Missions for Long-Term Partnerships." In *Engaging the Church: Analyzing the Canvas of Short-Term Missions*, edited by Laurie A. Fortunak and A. Scott Moreau, 110–14. Wheaton, IL: EMIS, 2008.

Rubin, Herbert J., and Irene Rubin. *Qualitative Interviewing: The Art of Hearing Data*. 2nd ed. Thousand Oaks: Sage, 2005.

Russell, Mark. "Missional Business Professionals: The Strategic and Practical Use of Business Professionals as Empowered Partners in Short-Term Missions." In *Effective Engagement in Short-Term Missions: Doing It Right!*, edited by Robert J. Priest, 340–68. Pasadena: William Carey Library, 2008.

Slimbach, Richard. "First, Do No Harm." In *Engaging the Church: Analyzing the Canvas of Short-Term Missions*, edited by Laurie A. Fortunak and A. Scott Moreau, 80–92. Wheaton, IL: EMIS, 2008.

———. "The Mindful Missioner." In *Effective Engagement in Short-Term Missions: Doing It Right!*, edited by Robert J. Priest, 152–83. Pasadena: William Carey Library, 2008.

Smith, Alex G. "Evaluating Short-Term Missions: Missiological Questions." In *Effective Engagement in Short-Term Missions: Doing It Right!*, edited by Robert J. Priest, 34–61. Pasadena: William Carey Library, 2008.

Smith, Steve, and Ying Kai. *T4t: A Discipleship Re-Revolution*. Monument: WIGTake Resources, 2011.

Spradley, James P. *The Ethnographic Interview*. New York: Holt, Rinehart and Winston, 1979.

———. *Participant Observation*. New York: Holt, Rinehart and Winston, 1980.

Bibliography

Vella, Jane. *Learning to Listen, Learning to Teach: The Power of Dialogue in Educating Adults*. The Jossey-Bass Higher and Adult Education Series. San Francisco: Jossey-Bass, 2002.

Ver Beek, Kurt Alan. "Lessons from the Sapling: Review of Quantitative Research on Short-Term Missions." In *Effective Engagement in Short-Term Missions: Doing It Right!*, edited by Robert J. Priest, 474–502. Pasadena: William Carey Library, 2008.

Wan, Enoch, and Geoffrey Hartt. "Complementary Aspects of Short-Term Missions and Long-Term Missions: Case Studies for a Win-Win Situation." In *Effective Engagement in Short-Term Missions: Doing It Right!*, edited by Robert J. Priest, 62–98. Pasadena: William Carey Library, 2008.

Wan, Enoch Yee-nock. *Diaspora Missiology: Theory, Methodology, and Practice*. Portland: Institute of Diaspora Studies: Western Seminary, 2011.

Werner, Roland, et al. *Day of Devastation, Day of Contentment: The History of the Sudanese Church across 2000 Years*. Nairobi, Kenya: Paulines Publications Africa, 2000.

Wilder, Michael S., and Shane W. Parker. *Transformission: Making Disciples through Short-Term Missions*. Nashville: B&H, 2010.

Ybarrola, Dr. Steven J. "Avoiding the Ugly Missionary Anthropology and Short-Term Missions." In *Effective Engagement in Short-Term Missions: Doing It Right!*, edited by Robert J. Priest, 100–119. Pasadena: William Carey Library, 2008.

Zehner, Edwin. "On the Rhetoric of Short-Term Missions Appeals, with Some Practical Suggestions for Team Leaders." In *Effective Engagement in Short-Term Missions: Doing It Right!*, edited by Robert J. Priest, 184–207. Pasadena: William Carey Library, 2008.